COLLECTOR'S STYLE GUIDE

ARTS AND CRAFTS

Malcolm Haslam
was a dealer in decorative arts for four
years, and is a regular contributor to
antiques magazines. He is the author of
*Pottery, English Art Pottery 1865–1915,
Marks and Monograms of the Modern
Movement 1875–1930, The Real World of
the Surrealists, William Staite Murray* and
The Martin Brothers, Potters, and
co-author of *In the Deco Style* and
The Amazing Bugattis.

COLLECTOR'S STYLE GUIDE

ARTS AND CRAFTS

Malcolm Haslam

Ballantine Books • New York

All rights reserved under International and Pan-American Copyright
Conventions. Published in the United States by Ballantine Books, a division
of Random House, Inc., New York, and simultaneously in Canada by
Random House of Canada Limited, Toronto.
Originally published in Great Britain in 1988 by Macdonald & Co. Ltd.,
London.

Library of Congress Catalog Card Number: 88–091995

ISBN: 0-345-35936-4

Cover design by Richard Aquan
Manufactured in Italy
First American Edition: February 1989
10 9 8 7 6 5 4 3 2 1

ACKNOWLEDGEMENTS
I would like to thank the following for their help: Michael Carey and Al Grayson of Michael
Carey Inc.; Stanley Litchens; Pamala Douglas of E. Joseph; John Jesse & Irina Laski; Paul
Reeves; Michael Whiteway of Haslam & Whiteway; Phillips; and Sotheby's.
Malcolm Haslam

Picture credits for the Introduction
p.6–9 Mary Evans Picture Library; p.20 National Gallery, London; p.11 Royal Commission
for Historical Monuments; p.10 Victoria and Albert Museum, London; p.14 Mansell
Collection Ltd.; p.13 Glasgow School of Art Collection; p.19 British Architectural Library,
Drawings, RIBA, London; p.15 Arcaid/Richard Bryant; p.17 Victoria and Albert Museum;
p.21 Mary Evans Picture Library; p.49, 61, 72 and 74 courtesy of Artsman; p.52, 107 and 122
courtesy of Artsman (photographer Rick Echelmeyer).

Author's note on the Price Lists
The price lists are based on auction prices recorded during the last two years in European
and American salerooms. For the purposes of the lists £1 = $1.75.
The price band given is only a guide. If an item is found which is priced below the lower price
given, collectors should make sure that it is genuine, and not damaged or restored. If, on the
other hand, the price being asked is higher than the top price given in the list, collectors
should ask themselves if the object is of particularly fine quality, particularly large of its sort,
very rare, or has some other exceptional feature.
The figure indicating quality of design and/or decoration is largely subjective, and the
collector will no doubt find it entertaining to compare his/her own taste with the author's.

CONTENTS

INTRODUCTION

Thomas Carlyle.

The term 'Arts and Crafts' does not define an artistic style as 'Art Deco' and 'Art Nouveau' do; although there are some visual motifs which characterize Arts and Crafts objects, the same motifs may be found on objects which are definitely not Arts and Crafts. The expression refers rather to an attitude, or a set of attitudes, in the mind of a designer, an artist or a craftsman, involving not only art but also society, and the interaction between the two.

The ideas behind the Arts and Crafts movement had more to do with the creation of the art-object than with the art-object itself. Several Arts and Crafts objects even bear the evidence of this concern with the processes of manufacture: for instance, the hammer marks on beaten copper or silver were often left clearly visible, and mortise and tenon joints or dovetailing were exposed and made into prominent features of some furniture. As well as producing decorative effects, such details were intended to proclaim loudly that the object had been made by a craftsman using nothing but his hands and the simplest tools.

REBELLING AGAINST THE MACHINE

Ever since the Industrial Revolution there has been in Western thinking an element of rebellion against the tyranny of the machine. The philosopher Thomas Carlyle protested about the dehumanizing effects of machinery in his essay *Signs of the Times* published in 1829: 'Nothing is now done directly by hand; all is by rule and calculated contrivance .... On every hand, the living artisan is driven from his workshop, to make room for a speedier, inanimate one.

The shuttle drops from the fingers of the weaver, and falls into iron fingers that ply it faster.'

The author and critic John Ruskin borrowed many of Carlyle's ideas. In 1853 he published *Stones of Venice*, and the chapter entitled 'The Nature of Gothic' was to be a formative influence on most of the leading figures in the Arts and Crafts movement. Ruskin described the satisfaction felt by the medieval craftsman whose hand had been guided by his imagination to make artefacts of beauty and vitality; the machine, on the other hand, could produce only lifeless objects. Ruskin wrote: 'Men were not intended to work with the accuracy of tools, to be precise and perfect in all their actions. If you will have that precision out of them you must unhumanize them.'

John Ruskin.

Such abhorrence for machinery was shared by William Morris, whose attempts to practise what Ruskin had preached in 'The Nature of Gothic' helped to instigate the Arts and Crafts movement. Morris, however, realized that the machines themselves could be as much a blessing as a curse; the fault arose only when machines deprived people of work which could ennoble them and lighten their lives. 'If the necessary reasonable work be of a mechanical kind', he said, 'I must be helped to do it by a machine, not to cheapen my labour, but so that as little time as possible may be spent upon it.'

In the view of the Arts and Crafts movement the use of machinery was criminal when it undermined the dignity of human labour. As a result, objects produced by the movement were very expensive, being handmade. This riled Morris, who angrily – if rhetorically – asked: 'Why should I minister to the swinish luxury of the rich?' He well knew why. The explanation was spelt out by the artist Walter Crane, one of Morris's closest friends, who wrote: 'It should be remembered that cheapness in art and handicraft is well nigh impossible, save in some forms of more or less mechanical reproduction. In fact, cheapness . . . . in the sense of low-priced productions, can only be obtained at the cost of cheapness – that is, the cheapening of human life and labour . . . . Art is, in its true sense, after all, the crown and flowering of life and labour, and we cannot reasonably expect to gain that crown except at the true value of the human life and labour of which it is the result.' To the protagonist of the Arts and Crafts outlook, the sense of fulfilment experienced in practising a craft was more valuable than the

pleasure gained from the objects produced. It has often been claimed that the Arts and Crafts movement's attitude to the use of machinery was ambivalent; however, although complicated it was perfectly logical.

REVERENCE FOR THE MIDDLE AGES

Another attitude characteristic of the Arts and Crafts movement was disaffection with the conditions of life prevailing at the time. Crane blamed the difficulties which he described in the above quotation on 'present economic conditions', and Morris said that 'it is the allowing machines to be our masters and not our servants that so injures the beauty of life *nowadays*' (my italics). 'Apart from the desire to produce beautiful things', he said on another occasion, 'the leading passion of my life has been and is hatred of modern civilisation.' Ruskin, too, regarded prevailing conditions as particularly pernicious and asserted that 'the foundations of society were never yet shaken as they are at this day'. The very titles of two of Carlyle's works convey the same sentiment – *Signs of the Times* and *Past and Present*. In the latter book Carlyle criticized nineteenth-century society and compared it unfavourably with life and values in medieval times. Part of his inspiration probably came from a book written by the architect and designer A.W.N. Pugin in 1835, entitled *Contrasts: or a Parallel between the Noble Edifices of the Middle Ages, and Corresponding Buildings of the Present Day, shewing the Present Decay of Taste*.

The art and architecture of the thirteenth, fourteenth and fifteenth centuries became a shibboleth to the

William Morris, father of the Arts and Crafts movement.

St Jerome in his Study by Antonello da Messina, a painting of the Italian Renaissance in the National Gallery, London, which was admired by members of the Arts and Crafts movement in England.

Holy Trinity church, Sloane Street, London, designed by J.D. Sedding.

Arts and Crafts movement, although different personalities favoured different aspects of medieval culture. Many found their ideal in the donnish humanism of the Renaissance. Both Halsey Ricardo (an architect closely associated with the Arts and Crafts movement) and William Lethaby (one of its most prominent figures) cited the chamber shown in the painting *St Jerome in his Study* by Antonello da Messina as an example of the well-furnished room. 'The Saint gets all he can properly want,' wrote Ricardo, 'and he gets over and above .... the look of peace and calm in his room, that can so seldom be found with us.' Lethaby evinced the same yearning for a paradise lost in his comments on the painting. 'Compare', he wrote, 'the dignity of serene and satisfying order with the most beautifully furnished room you know; how vulgar our good taste appears and how foreign to the end of culture – Peace.' A glimpse of this serenity so craved by the Arts and Crafts soul comes through in a wood engraving of an interior at Kelmscott Manor, Morris's house in the Cotswolds.

11

If St Jerome's study was a painted dream, the Gothic architecture of Britain and France was a very accessible reality. From tiny parish churches to great cathedrals, examples of the Gothic craftsmanship extolled by Ruskin were everywhere to hand. Many British designers of the Arts and Crafts movement spent the early part of their career working in an architect's office. There they were expected to make themselves conversant with Gothic architecture and decoration, and they often went on walking tours, in Britain or France, sketching the towers and spires, corbels and gargoyles of medieval buildings.

Just as the protagonists of the Arts and Crafts movement have sometimes been falsely accused of a Luddite attitude to machines, so have they been blamed for wilfully turning away from modern life and burying themselves in the romantic world of the Middle Ages. But in fact they subscribed to a healthy scepticism about the medieval era, a scepticism expressed strongly by Ruskin: 'We don't want either the life or the decorations of the thirteenth century back again . . . . All that gorgeousness of the Middle Ages, beautiful as it sounds in description, noble as in many respects it was in reality, had, nevertheless, for foundation and for end, nothing but the pride of life – the pride of the so-called superior classes; a pride which supported itself by violence and robbery, and led in the end to the destruction both of the arts themselves and the States in which they flourished.' When William Morris wrote about a medieval utopia, he entitled the book *News from Nowhere*, thus implicitly acknowledging that such a place had never existed.

ARTS AND CRAFTS AND PRESERVATION

The reverence for the art and architecture of the Middle Ages shown by Morris and other leading figures of the Arts and Crafts movement was translated into a very practical endeavour. In 1877 the Society for the Protection of Ancient Buildings was founded by Morris, and such luminaries of the movement as Philip Webb, William Lethaby and Ernest Gimson were among its most active members. The Society's efforts were directed towards the preservation of Gothic churches threatened with destruction or – as woeful a fate – so-called 'restoration'. Morris decided that he would no longer supply stained glass windows for old churches, only new ones, although this meant some loss of business. Soon the Society was trying to safeguard other old buildings besides Gothic churches, and it also campaigned for the preservation of buildings overseas that were threatened wth restoration. 'The less that can be done to an ancient building the better', was how the Committee of the Society expressed its guiding principle in 1881.

Today, when the importance of preserving not only our artistic heritage but also the landscape and wildlife is taken for granted, it is easy to forget the origins of such ideas. As well as trying to protect ancient architecture, the Arts and Crafts movement was involved in the earliest attempts to save the countryside from the ravages of industry and speculative building. 'Both the leaders and the led', declared Morris, 'are incapable of saving so much as half a dozen commons from the grasp of inexorable Commerce: . . . . less lucky

An interior at Kelmscott Manor, from a wood-engraving by E.H. New. 13

than King Midas, our green fields and clear waters, nay the very air we breathe, are turned not to gold .... but to dirt.' If these sentiments have a familiar ring, Morris's pessimistic vision of the end of mankind 'in a counting-house on the top of a cinder-heap' appears as vivid today as when he perceived it a hundred years ago.

In 1894 the National Trust was founded to acquire and administer areas of the English countryside and buildings of artistic or historic interest. Two figures who helped to establish the Trust were more or less connected with the Arts and Crafts movement. Octavia Hill had been an ardent disciple of Ruskin, and as a young woman she had wanted to be an artist. She had understood, however, the social implications of Ruskin's message and had devoted her energies to the provision of housing for the poor — housing which was beautified with tiles made by William de Morgan. Canon Rawnsley, the other figure actively engaged in the campaign to establish the National Trust, worked for many years to help the deprived inhabitants of the English Lake District and to preserve the natural beauty of their environment. In 1884 he founded an evening institute which became the Keswick School of Industrial Art. Classes in metalwork were held at this School, which produced a lot of very good Arts and Crafts copper and silver ware.

In America, Morris's injunctions to preserve the landscape were readily accepted by a generation reared on the writings of Ralph Waldo Emerson and Henry Thoreau. The latter's account of his life in the woods of Walden was calculated to imbue the reader's mind with both reverence

for nature and respect for the basic crafts of house-building. The American cabinetmaker Gustav Stickley declared that his highly influential magazine *The Craftsman* was intended 'to promote and extend the principles established by Morris', and in 1904 it reprinted his article 'Art and the Beauty of Earth'. The pages of *The Craftsman* are strewn with essays and aphorisms redolent of Thoreau's philosophy, for example 'In the Yosemite with John Muir', a hymn to the wilderness which helped towards the establishment of the valley as a National Park.

The writer Henry Thoreau, whose book *Walden* had a strong influence on the Arts and Crafts movement in America.

Library of the Glasgow School of Art; the building and all the furniture were designed by the Scottish architect Charles Rennie Mackintosh.

ARTS AND CRAFTS ORGANIZATIONS IN BRITAIN

In 1861, William Morris established his decorating business, at first called Morris, Marshall, Faulkner & Co., but in 1875 reorganized to become Morris & Co; it is often referred to as 'the Firm'. In 1881 the workshops were moved from central London to Merton Abbey, on the outskirts. The Firm made stained glass, furniture, tiles, wallpapers, fabrics, carpets and tapestries in which motifs of flora and fauna predominated. In 1877 showrooms were opened in Oxford Street, London, where, in addition to goods produced by the Firm, metalwork by W.A.S. Benson and pottery by William de Morgan were usually on sale.

In 1882 the Century Guild was started. It was a loose association between the architects Arthur Mackmurdo and Herbert Horne, the artist Selwyn Image, and the enamellist and stained-glass artist Clement Heaton. The Guild produced furniture, fabrics, metalwork and cloisonné enamels, and the magazine *The Hobby Horse* was issued intermittently between 1884 and 1892.

Many important figures of the Arts and Crafts movement in Britain started their careers as apprentices or assistants working in an architect's office. One of them was run by George Street; Morris worked there, as well as his close friend Philip Webb who supplied the Firm with designs. The architect John Sedding, himself a protégé of Street, took on as assistants Henry Wilson and John Paul Cooper, who both became silversmiths and jewellers, and Ernest Gimson, later a furniture designer. In the office of Richard Norman Shaw, yet another of Street's former assis-

tants, worked Sidney Barnsley, who became a cabinetmaker, and William Lethaby, perhaps the most influential figure of the Arts and Crafts movement after Morris.

At the social gatherings of these architectural assistants the Art Workers' Guild was conceived. It was established in 1884 and four years later spawned the Arts and Crafts Exhibition Society. The Art Workers' Guild, 'a spiritual oasis in the wilderness of modern life' as Henry Wilson called it, provided a forum where architects, artists, designers and craftsmen could exchange views and information. The shows organized by the Arts and Crafts Exhibition Society, at first held annually and then every three years, gave members an opportunity to display their wares and sell them to the public.

In 1888 Charles Robert Ashbee started the Guild of Handicraft in the East End of London. Furniture, metalwork and jewellery were made at the Guild's workshops, mostly to Ashbee's designs. There was a philanthropic element in Ashbee's enterprise, in that the Guildsmen were recruited from the locality, a depressed area of London with a high level of unemployment. In 1902 the Guild moved to the village of Chipping Campden in Gloucestershire, reinforcing the Arts and Crafts movement's links with the Cotswolds which had been originally forged when William Morris bought Kelmscott Manor in Oxfordshire, and was strengthened by Ernest Gimson and Sidney Barnsley who had both established workshops in the area.

In 1890 the Birmingham Guild of Handicraft was started by members of an evening-class run by Arthur Stansfield Dixon who became its chief designer. The Guild produced a wide range of metalwork and printed a magazine, *The Quest*, on its own press. The Arts and Crafts movement also blossomed in Birmingham at the School of Art and the Vittoria Street School for Jewellers and Silversmiths. Arthur Gaskin, who was headmaster of the latter from 1902, designed and made jewellery. In 1898 William Howson Taylor, son of the headmaster of the School of Art, opened the Ruskin Pottery at West Smethwick, a suburb of Birmingham.

In 1893 Francis H. Newbery, principal of the Glasgow School of Art, organized a series of lectures on the Arts and Crafts and so launched a flurry of activity in that city. The architect Charles Rennie Mackintosh and others developed what became known as the Glasgow style, which was more abstract and geometrical than English Arts and Crafts. The Glasgow designers created large amounts of furniture, metalwork, jewellery and needlework.

The metalworkers Nelson Dawson and Edward Spencer founded the Artificers' Guild in 1901 at Hammersmith, London. Two years later Dawson resigned and Spencer joined up with Montague Fordham, the owner of a West End gallery who had previously been a director of the Birmingham Guild of Handicraft. Spencer designed metalwork and jewellery which were made by the craftsmen of the Artificers' Guild. Fordham's gallery, which was also called the Artificers' Guild, sold not only the Guild's metalwork and jewellery but also jewellery by May Morris (William Morris's daughter), metalwork by Henry Wilson and John Paul Cooper, ceramics designed by Spencer and made at the Upchurch Pottery in Kent, and the salt-glazed stoneware pots and figures made by the Martin brothers.

In 1896 the Central School of Arts and Crafts was opened by the London County Council with William Lethaby and the sculptor George Frampton as joint directors. From 1902 to 1911 Lethaby was sole principal, and among the appointments that he made to the staff were many of the leading figures of the Arts and Crafts movement: Alexander Fisher, the metalworker, taught enamelling; George Jack, the chief furniture designer for Morris & Co. from about 1890, taught woodcarving and gilding; Edward Johnston taught calligraphy and illumination; Alfred Powell, who had been one of Sedding's assistants and decorated pottery for Wedgwood, taught painting on china; Henry Wilson taught drawing from the life.

In 1913 the Omega Workshops were opened by Roger Fry, artist and critic, in Fitzroy Square, London. The Workshops produced furniture, ceramics, fabrics and rugs designed and sometimes painted by leading avant-garde artists including Henri Gaudier-Brzeska, Duncan Grant, Vanessa Bell and Percy Wyndham Lewis. The Workshops carried out a

'Prairie School' house in Chicago, designed by Frank Lloyd Wright.

few schemes of interior decoration before they were closed in 1919.

INSTITUTIONS IN AMERICA

In the United States, the Arts and Crafts movement first stirred during the 1870s in Cincinnati, Ohio. The principal instigator was an Englishman, Benn Pitman, who had come to America in 1852 to promote the system of shorthand that had been devised by his brother Sir Isaac Pitman. At the University of Cincinnati School of Design, Benn Pitman started courses in woodcarving and china-painting which were largely attended by women from the wealthier middle classes. Notable among these were Mary Louise McLaughlin who made furniture and decorated pottery, and Maria Longworth Nichols who in 1880 founded the Rookwood Pottery.

In New York, Candace Wheeler was responsible for the foundation in 1877 of the Society of Decorative Art, which ran courses in various crafts including needlework and china-painting. Two years later Mrs Wheeler joined forces with Louis Comfort Tiffany in a decorating business called L.C. Tiffany and the Associated Artists, but in 1883 they split up and Associated Artists continued as an independent enterprise, producing textiles and needlework. L.C. Tiffany produced stained glass, jewellery, iridescent glass and pottery independently of his father's firm.

The Arts and Crafts movement was launched in Chicago towards the end of the 1880s. Frank Lloyd Wright and some other young architects who were working in the same office developed a sparsely decorated, geometrical style which they used not only in their architecture but also in designs for furniture, carpets, stained glass and other decorative objects. They and other Chicago architects and designers who adopted the style were collectively known as the Prairie School.

Another, quite independent, strand of the Arts and Crafts movement in Chicago was Hull House, a settlement started in 1889 by Jane Addams and Ellen Gates Starr in a poor district of the city. There instruction was offered in several crafts including metalwork, jewellery and bookbinding. In 1897 the Chicago Society of Arts and Crafts was established at Hull House, and Wright was among the founder members. From 1900 the talented silversmith and metalworker Robert Riddle Jarvie was a regular exhibitor at the Society's shows.

In 1895 the Roycroft Press was established at East Aurora, New York, by Elbert Hubbard, who was neither an artist nor a designer but an accomplished entrepreneur and publicist. Through his magazine *Philistine* he promoted the Roycroft books, which soon began to sell in large numbers. He then started a bindery and a leather workshop, and from 1897 was selling items of furniture. In 1909 he opened up an art copper department. Hubbard's regime of plain living combined with artistic creativity attracted many to the Roycroft community who were given employment in the various workshops. Among the most notable Roycrofters were the metalworker Karl Kipp, who later left to start his own venture, the Tookay Shop, and the designer Dard Hunter, who eventually set up his own press.

Gustav Stickley established his furniture business at Eastwood, near

18

Houses designed by C.R. Ashbee, from a watercolour by F.C. Varley.

Syracuse, New York, in 1898, after he returned from a visit to Europe where he had met C.R. Ashbee and other Arts and Crafts personalities. The simple oak furniture he designed and manufactured soon became very popular, but its style had less to do with British precedents than with the so-called 'Mission' furniture that was produced in America from the mid-1890s. Stickley followed Hubbard's example and promoted his furniture through his magazine *The Craftsman*, which he launched in 1901 and which became the mouthpiece of the American Arts and Crafts movement.

Ernest A. Batchelder was a frequent contributor to *The Craftsman*. He had studied in England at the Birmingham School of Art and in 1902 helped to establish the Handicraft Guild in Minneapolis. He taught at the Summer School there from 1903 to 1908. During that time, in 1904, he was appointed head of the department of Arts and Crafts at the Throop Polytechnic Institute (now the California Institute of Technology) in Pasadena, California. Through his teaching and his book *Design in Theory and Practice*, published in 1910, Batchelder had enormous influence on the later stages of the American Arts and Crafts movement, particularly on the West Coast. His main precept was the importance of practising the crafts. He followed it himself in 1909 when he opened a tile-works in Pasadena. 'We learn by doing', he declared.

Civilization in the United States was still young at the turn of the century and it must have been difficult for an American then to regret the disappearance of traditional crafts in a land where people looked forward rather than back. But in the course of the twentieth century, in the United States as much as in Britain, the Arts and Crafts movement has kept alive the desire for the handmade object. We may admire industrial design and be grateful for the efficiency and practicality of our

Stoneywell Cottage, Markfield, Leicestershire, built by the architect and designer Ernest Gimson as a summer home for his elder brother.

Elbert Hubbard and his wife, Alice; the chairs, desk and lamp are all products of the Roycroft workshops.

transport, our office equipment and our domestic appliances, but we still cherish the artefacts of the Arts and Crafts movement, both as objects of beauty and as solid mementos of a world where built-in obsolescence did not rule.

The Arts and Crafts movement has been seen as a stepping-stone between Victorian decorative art and modern design, but to take such a view is to impose on the minds of the men and women who took part in it, an historical pattern that was never there. The movement has been regarded as a failed experiment in socialism, a frustrated attempt to put into practice an ideal of co-operative enterprise, but to pass such a judge-ment is to weigh the endeavours of late nineteenth-century men and women on scales devised in the second half of the twentieth century. The most modest aim of the move-ment was to preserve traditional handicrafts in the same way that it tried to protect the countryside that nurtured those crafts, and the build-ings and objects that are their monu-ments. Its most magnificent aim was to provide men and women with work which satisfied their souls and left the world a more beautiful place. 'It would be as well if all of us', wrote Ruskin in 'The Nature of Gothic', 'were good handicraftsmen in some kind, and the dishonour of manual labour done away with altogether.' 21

CHAPTER ONE

FURNITURE
AND
TEXTILES

Morris & Co. printed cotton *Evenlode*
curtain. 80 × 220cm Haslam & Whiteway,
London. Price (pair): £625

From soon after Queen Victoria's accession (1837) furniture was made in Britain with characteristics of the style that, towards the end of the nineteenth century, became known as Arts and Crafts. By the 1850s some pieces of simple, oak furniture began to appear in people's homes and in a few institutional buildings. In contrast to most early Victorian furniture, these pieces were decorated with a minimum of carving and the strongest feature of their design was their construction, often visually emphasized by the use of mortise and tenon joints. Few elements were turned on the lathe; instead they were faceted or chamfered. Legs were not disguised as carvings of goddesses, vines or wolfhounds, nor were they hidden discreetly under skirts of brocade or damask. Such furniture had not been designed since the seventeenth century.

Oak side table
Height: 75cm
Sold: Phillips, London, 27/10/87
Price: £528

SIMPLICITY AND THE GOTHIC REVIVAL

Some of the first pieces of this new style of furniture were designed by the architect Augustus Welby Northmore Pugin. 'I am anxious', he wrote to his friend the cabinetmaker John G. Crace, 'to introduce a sensible style of furniture of good oak and *constructively* put together that will compete with the vile trash made and sold.' Pugin fulfilled this ambition, even though he died within a year or two of writing this letter.

Considerable quantities of this sort of furniture, designed in the Gothic style, were manufactured by Crace and by several firms, including Howard & Sons and Gillow's, during the 1850s, 1860s and 1870s. Not all of it has the quality of design that Pugin gave his furniture or the quality of construction on which he always insisted. It was usually made of oak, but sometimes of walnut with the handles of drawers and doors in brass. Pugin's son, Edward Welby, also designed some items of furniture. But although they were made of oak and simply constructed, often with prominent mortise and tenon joints, the designs were usually somewhat outlandish and mannered.

In 1853, the year following A.W.N. Pugin's death, the popularity of the Gothic revival in Victorian Britain was given a boost by the publication of John Ruskin's book *The Stones of Venice*. The chapter entitled 'The Nature of Gothic' was to become almost the manifesto of the Arts and Crafts movement, and was printed as a separate publication in 1892, by William Morris's Kelmscott Press. As Pugin had done, Ruskin emphasized simplicity of design and honesty in construction.

Several architects, notably George Edmund Street, John Pollard Seddon and William Burges, were swayed by Ruskin's ideas, and designed furniture as well as buildings in the neo-Gothic style. Street and Seddon both had family ties with cabinetmakers (Street's first wife was a close friend of Jessie Holland whose father William was a director of Holland & Sons, cabinetmakers, and two years after his wife's death, Street married Jessie Holland herself), and furniture to their designs was made in comparatively large quantities. Burges's furniture, however, often painted with elaborate pictorial decoration, is very rare and very expensive.

Street's furniture is commendable for the beauty of its proportions and the almost unadorned simplicity of its construction. It was usually made of oak, although sometimes pine was used. A lot of Street's furniture was made for buildings that he designed, including several churches and the Law Courts in London. Over the years, a considerable quantity of his work has found its way on to the art market, but it is nevertheless very expensive; even a single sidechair will stretch the average collector's budget.

Furniture designed by John Pollard Seddon is similar to Street's, both in style and in price. Seddon's father, Thomas, was one of London's leading cabinetmakers, and most of the furniture which John designed was manufactured by the family firm. John's brother, also called Thomas, was a landscape painter and a close associate of the Pre-Raphaelites, particularly Ford Madox Brown. When the younger Thomas Seddon started free art classes for his father's workmen, Brown was taken on to give instruction.

25

MORRIS & CO.

At the London International Exhibition held in 1862, furniture designed by John Seddon, some of it painted by Pre-Raphaelite artists, was shown together with work by Burges. The same display featured furniture and interior decoration made by a firm which had been started a year earlier – Morris, Marshall, Faulkner & Co. William Morris himself never designed any furniture, apart from a few early pieces for his own use. However, his company (reorganized in 1875 as Morris & Co., and generally known as 'the Firm') manufactured and sold large quantities of furniture.

At first most pieces were designed by the architect Philip Webb, whom Morris had met when they were both working in Street's office. Webb's style was strongly influenced by Street's furniture, although he developed a personal idiom characterized by a subtle manipulation of volumes, and a refined elaboration of structure. He gradually liberated his work from the domination of the neo-Gothic style and exploited a wide range of sources, including Japanese furniture forms. Ford Madox Brown also designed some bedroom furniture for Morris & Co. It was extremely simple, built from shaped planks and held together by mortise and tenon joints.

'Of all the specific minor improvements in common household objects due to Morris, the rush-bottomed Sussex chair perhaps takes the first place', wrote J.W. Mackail in his *Life of William Morris*, published in 1899. The piece was copied, with minor refinements, from a common type of country chair, of which the Firm manufactured several variants.

The basic design, with a row of vertical spindles in the back, was produced in single chair, armchair, corner chair and settee versions. A round-seated armchair, based on a French provincial prototype, with its back featuring a decorative motif of canes bent into the shape of a wheatsheaf, was designed by the painter Dante Gabriel Rossetti. Another round-seated chair, with the spindles in its back formed in a cross, was designed by Ford Madox Brown. All versions were rush-seated and usually made of ebonized wood. The chairs proved enormously popular and were often plagiarized. Another Morris & Co. product which sold well was the adjustable armchair. This was also based on a country prototype that had been found in a Sussex carpenter's shop by George Warrington Taylor, the Firm's business manager.

THE EASTLAKE STYLE

The ethos of simple, well-made furniture in the neo-Gothic style preached by Pugin, Ruskin and Morris was widely disseminated by Charles Locke Eastlake in his book *Hints on Household Taste in Furniture, Upholstery and Other Details* published in 1868. He pressed the case for furniture 'constructed in a plain and straightforward manner', and illustrated the book with his own designs. Its success in England was nothing compared with its triumph in America; no fewer than six editions were issued there over the following twelve years. Pieces of furniture more or less directly taken from Eastlake's designs appear from time to time in Britain, but in the United States, furniture in what soon became known as the Eastlake style is less rare.

**Morris & Co. mahogany table
designed by George Jack**
Height: 69cm
Paul Reeves, London
Price: £1000

**Morris & Co. rush-seated
armchair designed by
D.G. Rossetti**
Height: 88cm
Paul Reeves, London
Price: £350

Kenton & Co. mahogany shelves
Width: 68cm
Sold: Phillips, London, 24/3/87
Price: £462

In Cincinnati, particularly, the Eastlake style was adopted by many furniture-makers — professional, semi-professional and amateur. Even before the appearance of Eastlake's book in America, Joseph Longworth, who helped to establish the Cincinnati Art Museum and the Art Academy of Cincinnati, commissioned the English woodcarver Henry Fry and his son William Henry to decorate the interior of a house that he had built for his daughter Maria (who was to found the Rookwood Pottery some years later). Before leaving England, Henry Fry had worked for Pugin and G.G. Scott, another Gothic Revival architect. Maria Longworth and her friends were so impressed by the Frys' work that in 1872 they persuaded the craftsmen to give them lessons. The following year a woodcarving department was established in the School of Design at the University of Cincinnati. The students, mostly ladies from the best Cincinnati families, made quantities of furniture, much of which was in the Eastlake style.

The cabinetmaker Isaac E. Scott also made furniture in the Eastlake style. Born near Philadelphia, Scott worked in Chicago during the 1870s. There he carried out a number of commissions for John Glessner, a wealthy Chicago businessman whose wife Frances took a lively interest in the Arts and Crafts (she was subsequently to become an accomplished silversmith herself).

Two other firms of cabinetmakers, Daniel Pabst of Philadelphia and Herter Brothers of New York, manufactured furniture in styles related to Eastlake's designs, but it was generally too elaborate and ornate to be properly considered part of the Arts and Crafts tradition.

THE QUEEN ANNE REVIVAL

In Britain during the 1870s, the Queen Anne style was revived by many architects, most notably Richard Norman Shaw. He had succeeded Webb as Street's chief assistant, and had earlier designed a few pieces of neo-Gothic furniture. When he designed the Bedford Park estate in London, with houses built in the Queen Anne style, he also designed a rush-seated, oak armchair based on an early eighteenth-century original. These chairs provided seating at the Tabard Inn, the estate's hostelry; they were also sold to the general public through Morris & Co. In 1882 Shaw designed further items of furniture in an eighteenth-century style, which were made by W.H. Lascelles at the Finsbury Steam Joinery Works.

The style of the furniture that the architect Arthur Heygate Mackmurdo designed for the Century Guild, founded in 1882, was also derived from eighteenth-century architecture and furniture. In his furniture, Mackmurdo made a special feature of the wide cornice which had been used extensively in architecture by Wren and his followers, but he pared it down until it became a flat, horizontal element, which he often incorporated as the terminal to an upright. This device was widely used by designers of Arts and Crafts furniture over the next twenty-five years. Most Century Guild furniture was manufactured by Collinson & Lock of London or Goodall's of Manchester.

Mackmurdo's enthusiasm for early eighteenth-century forms had been inspired, at least in part, by the direction in which Philip Webb's architecture had moved. Webb had developed a highly personal version of the Queen Anne style, which he used for most of the houses he built from the late 1870s onwards. In 1880 Webb took on an assistant, George Jack. Born in Long Island, USA, Jack had worked for architects in Glasgow and London before joining Webb. Towards the end of the 1880s he started designing furniture for Morris & Co., most of it in the eighteenth-century style made popular by the Queen Anne revival.

Many pieces designed by Jack were decorated with extensive marquetry, usually of flowers, and most were made in mahogany. The quality of craftsmanship was considerably higher than that found in furniture previously produced by Morris & Co., and these pieces were probably made at a workshop in Pimlico, London, which the Firm acquired in 1887 from Holland & Sons.

The metalworker W.A.S. Benson also designed some pieces of furniture for Morris & Co. in a style based on early eighteenth-century forms. They were made in mahogany and usually incorporated elaborate embellishments in cast brass. Previously, Benson had designed some very simple bedroom furniture in oak for Morris & Co., which was shown in 1884 at an exhibition in Manchester.

The American architect Henry Hobson Richardson, who had designed some furniture in the Eastlake style during the 1870s, visited William Morris in 1882 and spent half a day with him inspecting the Firm's workshops at Merton Abbey near London. On his return to the United States, Richardson built the Converse Memorial Library in Malden, Massachusetts, in a style related to the Queen Anne revival. He also designed a chair for the Library which combined features of eighteenth-century furniture and elements of the traditional Windsor chair. It was manufactured by the firm of A.H. Davenport & Co.

Walnut *prie dieu* designed by Ernest Gimson
Height: 101.5cm
Paul Reeves, London
Price: £650

Oak ladderback chair designed by Ernest Gimson
Height: 106cm
Paul Reeves, London
Price: £380

In Britain, with the foundation of the Art Workers' Guild in 1884 and the establishment of the Arts and Crafts Exhibition Society four years later, the movement began to assume a distinct identity and to enlist widespread support among both artists and patrons. In 1888 Charles Robert Ashbee started his Guild of Handicraft in the East End of London which was soon producing pieces of furniture in the style of the Queen Anne revival, often decorated with painted and gilt gesso.

THE COTSWOLD SCHOOL

In 1890 a furniture-making company was set up called Kenton & Co. Among its founders were three young architects: Ernest Gimson, who was articled to J.D. Sedding whose office was next door to Morris & Co. in Oxford Street, and William Lethaby and Sidney Barnsley, who were both assistants to Richard Norman Shaw. They took premises, hired some professional cabinetmakers and produced furniture which was usually made of mahogany or oak, often decorated with inlay. But the firm lasted only two years, and pieces of Kenton & Co. furniture are rare.

After the break-up of Kenton & Co. Lethaby designed only a limited amount of furniture, usually in connection with the few architectural commissions which he undertook. Gimson and Barnsley, however, devoted the rest of their lives to the production of fine furniture, although Gimson also practised as an architect. They set up independent workshops at Sapperton, a village in the Cotswolds. Gimson designed furniture which was made by a team of skilled carpenters; oak, walnut, black and brown ebony were the woods mostly used.

Pieces of Gimson's furniture are either very plain, or else decorated with quite elaborate inlays of holly, fruitwoods, ivory, abalone shell, mother-of-pearl and silver. A few were painted with floral designs by Alfred Powell the architect and pottery decorator. Typical features are decorative chamfering and exposed mortise and tenon joints. Gimson paid homage to Morris by designing another variant of the rush-seated country chair; his version has three long spindles in the back.

After Gimson's death in 1919, furniture continued to be made to his designs by Peter Waals, a Dutchman who had been taken on by Gimson as foreman in 1900 and who set up his own workshop in 1920 at Chalford.

Sidney Barnsley was a man of reserved character, and his austere furniture reflects its maker's temperament. He not only designed his oak furniture, he also made it. By observation and imitation Barnsley

**Cuban mahogany serving table
by Gordon Russell**
Height: 89cm
Paul Reeves, London
Price: £950

Walnut armchair
Height: 90cm
Sold: Phillips, London, 27/10/87
Price: £330

learnt the necessary skills and became a highly accomplished wood-worker. He regarded fine craftsman-ship as a matter of personal integrity; a compromise with quality was tan-tamount to dishonesty. Consequent-ly, pieces of his furniture were always well made. They are generally plain, sometimes decorated with simple gouged ornament, and oc-casionally feature some inlay.

The last member of the Cotswold School was Gordon Russell, who opened his furniture workshops at Broadway, Worcestershire after the First World War. This enterprise was run on more commercial lines than either Gimson or Barnsley would have countenanced. Russell designed pieces in a variety of styles ranging from Art Deco to country traditional; rush-seated ladder-back chairs were a speciality of the company. Oak, mahogany, yew, walnut and other, more exotic woods were used. Rus-sell's furniture is more available and cheaper than the work of either Gimson or Barnsley, which tends to be prohibitively expensive, especially the more ornate pieces.

VOYSEY AND SPOONER

With the removal of Gimson and Barnsley to the Cotswolds in the early 1890s, the centre of the London stage was filled by the Wood Handi-crafts Society which showed furni-ture designed by the architects Charles Francis Annesley Voysey and Charles Spooner at the Arts and Crafts Exhibitions of 1893 and 1896. Spooner involved himself in the actual making of the furniture that he designed; Voysey was only a des-igner. The Wood Handicrafts Society was run from Spooner's home in Hammersmith, London, but does not seem to have lasted more than a few years. Later, in association with the architect and craftsman Arthur Penty, Spooner started Elmdon & Co., which exhibited furniture at the Alpine Club in 1905. That enterprise, too, seems to have been short-lived, for in 1910 Spooner was involved in the Hampshire House Workshops, which were also located in Hammer-smith. Most of the furniture produced there was designed by him.

Spooner's furniture, like that of Kenton & Co. and the Cotswold School, was derived from a wide variety of traditional forms, ranging from medieval tables to the six-teenth-century Spanish *vargueno* (a chest mounted on a stand) particu-larly favoured by Gimson, and Queen Anne cupboards. Voysey's designs, however, were almost entirely in-novative. A lady's work cabinet designed by Voysey for the Wood Handicrafts Society and exhibited in 1893 represents a turning point in the development of Arts and Crafts furniture. Its broad, flat cornice may reflect Voysey's brief association during the 1880s with Mackmurdo, but in every other respect the cabinet looks forward rather than back. It was made of stained oak which would become one of the materials most frequently used for Arts and Crafts furniture. It had large strap hinges of elaborately pierced and chased metalwork made by William Bain-bridge Reynolds; such hinges were to become a common feature of later furniture. Its tall, narrow and taper-ing uprights were a characteristic of C.F.A. Voysey's work and were later incorporated in furniture by several other designers.

Voysey's furniture was made by a number of different craftsmen includ-ing William Hall, who had previously worked for Kenton & Co. Apart from furniture designed for the houses and offices that he built, Voysey also supplied designs to commercial cabinetmakers and piano manufacturers. Probably because a love of music was characteristic of the sort of people whose taste favoured Arts and Crafts furniture, piano manufacturers were keen to commission designs from the leading exponents of the style. Bechstein, for instance, employed both Voysey and another architect, Walter Cave, whose style during the 1890s was very similar. For example, a rush-seated ladderback chair designed by Cave, made in walnut, has several Voyseyesque fea-

tures, although its sinuous curves relate it at the same time to Continental Art Nouveau.

BAILLIE SCOTT

For the piano manufacturers John Broadwood & Sons, Mackay Hugh Baillie Scott designed an oak case which won immediate and widespread acclaim. The case was for an upright piano and the part above the legs was enclosed in a rectangular box with two large doors opening laterally at the front. Broadwood manufactured many examples of this design, some of them with inlaid or painted decoration, others much

Broadwood & Sons oak piano designed by M.H. Baillie Scott
Height: 127cm
Sold: Sotheby's, London, 19/12/86
Price: £825

plainer, and in stained oak; many of them had decorative strap hinges in steel or brass.

Most of Baillie Scott's furniture was manufactured by the firm of J.P. White at the Pyghtle Works in Bedford. In 1902 White's issued a catalogue entitled *A Book of Furniture* which featured more than 120 designs by Baillie Scott. Some pieces were inlaid with stylized floral motifs, after which they were named – for instance, 'Daffodil Dresser' and 'Carnation Lily Rose Cabinet'.

In 1897 Baillie Scott was commissioned to redecorate and furnish the drawing room and dining room of the Grand-Ducal Palace at Darmstadt, Germany. Much of the furniture and metalwork for this project was made by craftsmen at Ashbee's Guild of Handicraft, and from about this time Ashbee's own furniture designs have a strong flavour of Baillie Scott's style. Eighteenth-century forms, such as ball-and-claw feet and deep entablatures, which had previously appeared on Guild furniture, were now almost eliminated. The cleaner lines and inlaid decoration that characterize pieces by Baillie Scott, and the metal embellishments often used by Voysey on his furniture, began to appear in Ashbee's designs.

Another architect, Edgar Wood, worked in a similar style. His furniture, made largely for the houses that he built in the Manchester area, was also decorated with inlay and metal-

work. In common with many other Arts and Crafts designers, Wood sometimes incorporated appropriate mottoes in the decoration: for example he would put 'Great men have ever loved repose' on the headboard of a bedstead. Another instance is an Arts and Crafts book cabinet which bears the inscription 'Studies serve for delight' in a beaten copper panel.

Liberty & Co. oak chair with copper mounts
Height: 121cm
Paul Reeves, London
Price (pair): £950

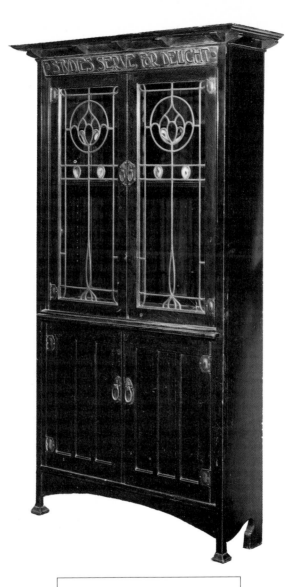

Ebonized oak book cabinet
Height: 213cm
Sold: Phillips, London, 18/6/87
Price: £528

SCOTTISH DESIGNERS

The novelty of Voysey's and Baillie Scott's furniture designs was taken many steps further by the Glasgow architect Charles Rennie Mackintosh. Of the Glasgow Four – Mackintosh, Herbert MacNair and their respective wives, the sisters Margaret and Frances Macdonald – only Mackintosh designed much furniture. The few pieces known to have been designed by MacNair are highly competent exercises in the English Arts and Crafts idiom, with only quite minor eccentricities in the Glasgow manner. Mackintosh's work, however, shows a virtuosity which is at once breathtaking and sometimes a little irritating.

It is easy to see why Mackintosh's furniture was not well received in England. Simplicity was sacrificed to sophistication, tradition was betrayed and there was scant respect for materials. His furniture was made out of a variety of woods including oak, cypress, pine and mahogany, but they have rarely been left untreated; they were either French polished, stained, ebonized or painted. Probably his most famous piece of furniture, the high-backed chair with a pierced oval backrail made for Miss Cranston's Argyle Street Tea Rooms, has only two tenuous links with the Arts and Crafts movement. First, there is a hint of Voysey's influence, particularly in the tall, tapering uprights, and second, there is the association with philanthropy – Miss Cranston opened her tearooms in an attempt to combat alcoholism. Mackintosh did design two versions of the traditional Windsor chair, almost as if he felt he ought to acknowledge his inheritance from the English Arts and Crafts movement.

George Walton preceded Mackintosh both as a student at the Glasgow School of Art and as a furniture designer and interior decorator working for Miss Cranston. For her Tea Rooms in Buchanan Street, Glasgow, Walton adapted a traditional Scottish chair, rush-seated, its arms curving forward from a narrow back pierced with a heart-shaped opening. This design was widely imitated, both in Britain and on the Continent. Otherwise, Walton's furniture is generally much more elegant; narrow, tapering legs which curve outwards are a typical feature. Allusions to the Glasgow style in his furniture designs are confined to a restrained use of geometrical forms such as the square and the sphere.

Beech armchair
Height: 87cm
Sold: Phillips, London, 21/10/86
Price (pair): £682

37

Another, more shadowy, Scottish furniture designer was Henry Wyse. He worked mainly in Arbroath and his furniture was made by a local cabinetmaker, William Middleton. Like much other Arts and Crafts furniture made in Scotland, Wyse's was usually ebonized or stained green, and decorated with copper mounts and panels of coloured glass. About 1900, with his friend Robert MacLaurin, Wyse started The Scottish Guild of Handicraft Ltd., which ran a gallery shop at 414 Sauciehall Street in Glasgow. His furniture was on sale at these premises, which were closed down in 1909. Wyse had turned his attention to pottery.

**William Birch oak armchair
designed by E.G. Punnett**
Height: 85.5cm
Sold: Sotheby's, London, 16/5/86
Price: £715

FURNITURE DESIGN IN CHICAGO

Recalling the 1890s, Frank Lloyd Wright wrote in 1957: 'Good William Morris and John Ruskin were much in evidence in Chicago intellectual circles at the time.' Walter Crane lectured at the Art Institute of Chicago in 1892, and through periodicals such as *The British Architect* and *International Studio* the city's architects and designers kept in touch with developments in Britain. The furniture designed by the architects of the Prairie School has points of similarity to the work of both Voysey and Mackintosh, but much of it was original. Wright's furniture has a rigid rectilinearity which relates it to some of Mackintosh's designs, but the American architect, shunning virtually all ornament, exploited the beauty of natural oak.

George Washington Maher worked during the late 1880s in the same architectural office as Wright. The furniture that he designed, however, at least until the turn of the century, is more ornate than Wright's; much of it was carved with recurring motifs such as lions, thistles or hollyhocks. Later, he adopted Wright's geometrical manner, occasionally softening its austerity with architectural forms akin to some of Voysey's.

Another Chicago architect, George Grant Elmslie, also worked in the same office as Wright and Maher, and then with Wright again in the office of the partnership Sullivan and Adler where in 1895 he became chief designer. His style was influenced by both Sullivan and Wright. The furniture he designed combines Wright's geometrical forms with Sullivan's organic, neo-Gothic ornament.

In 1900 the Chicago store of Marshall Field, which for many years had retailed Morris & Co. textiles and wallpapers, held a successful exhibition of furniture designed by Charles Rohlfs and made at his workshops in Buffalo, New York. Although often poorly constructed, Rohlfs's furniture, usually made of oak but sometimes of mahogany or ash, was finely carved with ornament in an Art Nouveau style. His work always shows great respect for 'The Grain of Wood', the title of an article that he contributed in 1901 to the magazine *House Beautiful*.

MISSION FURNITURE

The American furniture that is most essentially Arts and Crafts in character was called 'Mission' furniture. It is very plain and simple, generally

'Mission' oak armchair
Height: 87cm
Sold: Sotheby's, New York, 11/6/87
Price: $1430

made out of oak, and originally linked to furniture from the Franciscan missions in California. The principal exponents of the style were Gustav Stickley and the Roycroft Community, but it was first promoted by Joseph McHugh. During the 1890s McHugh ran his Popular Shop in New York selling Liberty furniture and metalwork, Morris & Co. chintzes and other imported goods. He was sent a simple, rush-seated chair from San Francisco, a replica of some found in the old Spanish missions. Soon he was selling similar chairs in the Popular Shop and manufacturing other pieces of furniture in the same style. In 1896 he took on a designer, Walter J.H. Dudley, whose work sometimes has great elegance but always retains the essential simplicity, as well as the stocky proportions of Mission furniture.

Gustav Stickley was one of five brothers who as boys all worked at their uncle's chair factory in Brandt, Pennsylvania. In 1898 he visited Europe and met several Arts and Crafts designers in Britain. On his return to the United States, he established the Gustav Stickley Company in Eastwood, near Syracuse, New York. This firm, which he first called 'United Crafts' and then 'Craftsman Workshops', he described as 'a guild of cabinetmakers, metal and leather workers, formed for the production of household furnishings'.

He became friendly with Irene Sargent, professor of art history and

Oak desk by Gustav Stickley
Height: 74cm
Sold: Sotheby's, New York, 5/12/86
Price: $1320

romance languages at Syracuse University, and she encouraged him to publish a monthly magazine *The Craftsman*, which propagated the Arts and Crafts philosophy and at the same time publicized Stickley's furniture. The magazine, issued from 1901 to 1916, gave its name to a style of architecture and interior decoration of which Mission furniture was an integral part. The Craftsman style became so popular that Stickley was selling his furniture through retail outlets across America, from Boston to Los Angeles. He seems to have designed nearly all the Craftsman furniture himself. Some pieces designed in 1903 by the artist Harvey Ellis are decorated with inlay, usually in fruitwood, copper and pewter; the floral motifs are related to designs by Baillie Scott and Mackintosh.

Craftsman furniture is well proportioned and beautifully made. In 1909 Stickley wrote: 'When I first began to use the severely plain, structural forms, I chose oak as the wood that, above all others, was adapted to massive simplicity of construction. The strong, straight lines and plain surfaces of the furniture follow and emphasize the grain and growth of the wood, drawing attention to, instead of destroying, the natural character that belonged to the growing tree.'

Furniture was first made by the Roycroft Community in 1896, when Elbert Hubbard decided to expand the community's buildings in East Aurora, New York. Visitors liked the furniture and wanted to buy pieces, so Hubbard, never one to miss a commercial opportunity, set about meeting the demand. Santiago Cadzow, one of the first cabinetmakers at Roycroft, designed some of the furniture and taught woodworking

skills to other Roycrofters. Designs for furniture were also provided by Victor Toothaker, an illustrator who drew room-settings for Hubbard's publications. The furniture was made in oak, ash or mahogany and many pieces have copper fittings. It is plain and often has prominent mortise and tenon joints. Some pieces have tapering legs ending in bulbous feet, a characteristic of much British Arts and Crafts furniture, in particular a very plain oak desk designed by Mackmurdo. In 1897 this desk was illustrated in *Studio* and it may well have been a significant influence on many designs for Mission furniture.

Another community, that of Rose Valley, founded by the architect Will Price in 1901 and situated in abandoned mills 2½ km (1½ miles) from

Ashtray by Gustav Stickley
Height: 70cm
Michael Carey Inc., New York
Price: $1200

41

the centre of Philadelphia, produced oak furniture, often featuring prominent mortise and tenon joints. But, unlike most Mission furniture, it is heavily carved, usually in a Gothic, Renaissance or colonial style.

Louis B. Easton, who married Elbert Hubbard's sister Jane, taught manual arts at Lemont High School in Illinois. In the evenings he built furniture of oak and leather to his own designs, some examples of which were shown in 1903 in an exhibition held at the Art Institute of Chicago. By that time, because of his poor health, Easton had taken his family to Pasadena, California. There

**Rush-seated oak chair
by Gustav Stickley**
Height: 106cm
Michael Carey Inc., New York
Price: $1500

Oak chair by Gustav Stickley
Height: 112cm
Michael Carey Inc., New York
Price: $750

he set himself up as a designer of bungalows and furniture. His rigidly rectilinear furniture was made of the local redwood and the construction was always heavily emphasized.

The brothers Charles Sumner Greene and Henry Mather Greene also settled in Pasadena, in 1893, and set up a small architectural practice. From 1907 Charles designed furniture for a number of the houses that they built. Although some pieces resemble Mission furniture, the Greene's work was influenced by Oriental design. It was made by the Peter Hall Manufacturing

Company of Pasadena. The construction was much more sophisticated than that of Mission furniture, and the materials used – usually mahogany, sometimes with ebony, fruitwood, silver and gemstones inlaid – were very much more exotic.

Some of the rush-seated chairs and oak cabinets produced by the Furniture Shop in San Francisco, California, owe something to the Craftsman style. The Furniture Shop was started after the earthquake and fire of 1906, by husband and wife Arthur and Lucia Mathews, artists who both painted in a style largely derived from Puvis de Chavannes and Whistler. They employed between

**Oak ladderback chair
by Gustav Stickley**
Height: 105.5cm
Michael Carey Inc., New York
Price: $500

Oak armchair by Gustav Stickley
Height: 101cm
Michael Carey Inc., New York
Price: $900

thirty and fifty craftsmen to carry out decorative schemes and build furniture which was then incised, painted and gilded with figures and flowers by Lucia Mathews. The furniture was designed by Arthur Mathews and his assistant Thomas A. McGlynn. Pieces made and decorated at the Furniture Shop are extremely rare today; few have survived in anything like their pristine condition.

Nearly all the American furniture described so far is very expensive. Even an umbrella stand by Gustav Stickley fetches hundreds of dollars in the saleroom. There is, however, a

43

considerable amount of Mission furniture which was made either by amateur woodworkers or by commercial manufacturers, and which is less expensive. In 1909 a book entitled *Mission Furniture: How to Make It* was written by H.H. Windsor, and was one of several similar manuals, and although many of their readers' attempts must have failed miserably, there are certainly appreciable quantities of homemade Mission furniture still existing today. Unfortunately, though, the large majority of pieces have little merit beyond a certain period charm.

**Oak umbrella stand
by Gustav Stickley**
Height: 92cm
Michael Carey Inc., New York
Price: $800

**Oak plant stand
by Gustav Stickley**
Height: 74.5cm
Michael Carey Inc., New York
Price: $1500

Oak tabouret by Gustav Stickley
Height: 52cm
Michael Carey Inc., New York
Price: $1000

Roycroft oak chair
Height: 105.5cm
Michael Carey Inc., New York
Price: $1500

COMMERCIAL CABINETMAKERS

The commercial cabinetmakers who produced Mission furniture included L. & G.J. Stickley, a company founded by two of Gustav's brothers in 1902 at Fayetteville, New York, and Stickley Brothers, another concern run by two of Gustav's siblings at Grand Rapids, Michigan. Grand Rapids was the chief furniture-manufacturing city in the United States and several firms there included Mission furniture as one of the lines which they were offering during the first two decades of this century. One of them was the Phoenix Furniture Company where David Wolcott Kendall was chief designer; others were the Sligh Furniture Company, the Michigan Chair Company, the Grand Rapids Furniture Manufacturing Company (which offered 'homebuilt arts and crafts furniture' in kits), and the Charles P. Limbert Company. In Chicago there was the Tobey Furniture Company and in New York the Majestic Furniture Company, both of which supplied Arts and Crafts furniture as well as more traditional lines. 45

In Britain, too, the Arts and Crafts furniture which is more affordable today was manufactured by commercial cabinetmakers. Timms & Webb were typical. They issued a catalogue in 1904 entitled *Thirty-Five Styles of Furniture*, one of which, 'British New

Oak rocking-chair
Height: 101cm
Michael Carey Inc., New York
Price: $1500

**Oak occasional table
by L. & J.G. Stickley**
Height: 83cm
Michael Carey Inc., New York
Price: $800

Oak table by L. & J.G. Stickley
Height: 74cm
Sold: Sotheby's, New York, 5/12/86
Price: $990

Art', reflected the furniture of the Arts and Crafts movement. Other firms specialized in Arts and Crafts furniture. Liberty & Co. produced stained oak furniture, often decorated with repoussé copper panels, fruitwood, metal and mother-of-pearl inlay. This furniture was designed either by artists on their own staff, such as Leonard Wyburd, or by freelance designers such as George Walton. Much of the furniture retailed by Liberty's was manufactured by the firm of William Birch at High Wycombe, Buckinghamshire, and some of it was designed by E.G. Punnett who worked for Birch.

47

William Birch oak armchair
Height: 84.5cm
Paul Reeves, London
Price: £750

The cabinetmakers Wylie & Lochhead of Glasgow started to produce furniture in a style strongly influenced by Mackintosh's designs. It was usually made in oak, mahogany or maple and designed by Ernest Archibald Taylor, George Logan or John Ednie. A few designs were also commissioned from Baillie Scott. Wylie & Lochhead furniture was often decorated with inlaid fruitwood, opals, coloured glass, enamels, tin or aluminium, and it was sometimes stained unusual tints such as grey or violet.

John Sollie Henry's firm made furniture in a similar style to Wylie & Lochhead. Henry established his company at 287–289 Old Street, London, apparently to make specifically Arts and Crafts style furniture, or 'Quaint and artistic furniture' as it was described in his advertisements. Mahogany was mainly used, and Henry himself did much of the designing. However, he also commissioned designs from Voysey, Benson and Walton, and made several pieces of furniture to designs by George Montague Ellwood, a founder member of the Guild of Art Craftsmen. Ellwood was awarded a medal for the furniture exhibited by Henry at the Paris Exhibition of 1900.

Heal & Son of London had been manufacturing furniture for more than eighty years when Ambrose Heal joined the firm in 1893. He designed a wide range of furniture in the Arts and Crafts style, and in 1899 the firm issued a catalogue of 'Simple Furniture'. Much of Ambrose Heal's furniture reflects the work of the Cotswold School; it was usually made of oak, although chestnut and mahogany versions were offered by the firm. In 1915 Heal became one of the founders of the Design and Industry Association; another was Harry Peach, proprietor of the Dryad Works in Leicester. This enterprise had been started in 1907 to manufacture cane and wicker furniture. The chief designer was Benjamin J. Fletcher, headmaster of the Leicester School of Art. His style contained elements of the German and Austrian cane furniture illustrated in *Studio*, but Dryad products have a look which is readily identifiable with the Arts and Crafts movement in England. Considerable quantities of Dryad cane and wicker furniture was exported to the United States.

**Oak tabouret
by Michigan Chair Company**
Height: 51cm
Sold: Phillips, New York, 27/6/87
Price: $825

**Heal's oak cabinet designed
by Ambrose Heal**
Height: 163cm
Sold: Phillips, London, 24/3/87
Price: £880

**Heal's oak table, inlaid
decoration**
Height: 70cm
Paul Reeves, London
Price: £325

**Heal's oak dressing table
and mirror**
Height: 134cm
Paul Reeves, London
Price: £450

In 1913 Roger Fry established the Omega Workshops at 33 Fitzroy Square, London. Omega artists, among whom were the painters Vanessa Bell, Duncan Grant and Wyndham Lewis (until 1915), designed pieces of furniture which were made by one or other of the numerous cabinetmakers in the area. On Tottenham Court Road, a stone's throw from Fitzroy Square, were several of the leading furniture stores (including Heal's) and many craftsmen had their own small workshops in the locality. One such was John Joseph Kallenborn, a Pole who worked for Ambrose Heal. He made the marquetry with which some of the best Omega furniture was decorated. A successful Omega design was a dining chair with a cane seat and back, and a backrail in the form of the Greek letter 'omega'. These chairs were made for Fry by the Dryad Works.

Much of the furniture was painted by the artists of the Omega Workshops in Post-expressionist styles. Arts and Crafts furniture had turned full circle, back to the early years of Morris & Co. when artists such as Rossetti and Burne-Jones had painted pieces of furniture in the avant-garde style of the day.

TEXTILES

Among the textiles of the Arts and Crafts movement in Britain and the United States, the greatest in number and the most varied in form were the embroideries. These were produced by hosts of amateurs as well as a few professionals. Table-cloths, napkins, runners, screens, firescreens and panels are to be found, embroidered with designs more or less in the Arts and Crafts style.

BRITISH EMBROIDERY

From about 1870 Morris & Co. sold embroideries designed by William Morris, his daughter May, Edward Burne-Jones and John Henry Dearle, and worked by Mrs Morris, May Morris and a second daughter Jenny, Catherine Holiday (the wife of the artist and designer Henry Holiday) and others. Their embroideries were close to the style of the firm's fabrics and wallpapers.

The School of Needlework (subsequently 'Royal') was founded in 1872 at South Kensington, London, and commissioned designs from such prominent Arts and Crafts designers as Morris, Burne-Jones, Walter Crane, Selwyn Image and Alexander Fisher. In 1879 the Leek Embroidery Society was founded by Mrs Thomas Wardle, wife of the owner of Wardle & Co., the Staffordshire firm where Morris's earliest chintzes were printed. The architects Richard Norman Shaw and J.D. Sedding de-

signed embroideries which were worked by members of the Society.

SCOTTISH EMBROIDERERS

In Scotland, Jessie Newbery, wife of Francis Newbery the principal of the Glasgow School of Art, taught embroidery at the school between 1894 and 1908, and did a great deal of it herself. Ann Macbeth who was also on the staff, and who wrote *Educational Needlecraft*, designed and worked embroideries which often incorporated glass beads. The artist, craftsman and poet Godfrey Blount designed embroidered hangings which usually featured stylized flowers and plants. They were made by the Haslemere Peasant Industries (which he founded in 1896); one of

Embroidered linen hanging
Height: 175cm
Sold: Phillips, New York, 27/6/87
Price: $979

them was exhibited by Wylie & Loch-head at Glasgow in 1901. Mary J. Newill who was associated with the Bromsgrove Guild of Handicraft, Christine Drummond Angus, Therese Lessore (the painter Walter Sickert's second and third wives respectively) and Phoebe Traquair all designed and worked embroideries of higher than average quality.

AMERICAN EMBROIDERY

In America, Candace Wheeler who taught at Cooper Union and other art schools in New York, and who was one of Louis Comfort Tiffany's partners in Associated Artists, the firm of interior decorators founded in 1879, helped to create a vogue for embroidering among middle-class American women during the last quarter of the nineteenth century. Particularly characteristic of her work, and that of her legion followers, was the combination of embroidery with block printing. The style of her work was derived from the floral patterns designed by William Morris.

All over America embroidery societies were formed. More successful than many was the Society of Blue and White Needlework which was run by the artists Ellen Miller and Margaret Whiting at Deerfield, Massachusetts, from 1896 to 1926. At first they made designs based on colonial patterns which were worked in blue and white linen yarns by the Society's members. Soon other colours were used and the designs became more innovative.

The ladies of Newcomb College, New Orleans, made embroideries in the style of the decoration featured on their pottery. Some of their embroidery was worked on their own hand-spun and hand-woven fabrics.

HAND-WOVEN FABRICS

Hand-woven textiles, carpets, rugs and tapestries were a prominent feature of Arts and Crafts exhibitions on both sides of the Atlantic. In America, many local Arts and Crafts societies included some sort of weaving among their activities. Rag rugs were always popular, and imitations of Indian blankets were made in numbers. The work of Edward Worst and Lucy Morgan was at a more sophisticated level. At the end of the First World War they founded the Penland School of Handicrafts in North Carolina. Worst revived the patterns of colonial coverlets, which are based on the structure of the weave.

The revival of hand-loom weaving in Britain dates from 1883 when Albert Fleming started the Langdale Weaving Industry in the Lake District, which produced plain and simple cloths. In London, Morris & Co. operated its own looms to weave textiles, tapestries, rugs and carpets. Most of these were designed by William Morris, but Burne-Jones and Walter Crane supplied some designs for tapestries. John Henry Dearle designed some tapestry backgrounds and borders, and a few of the later textiles. Annie Garnett, at her Windermere Spinnery, also in the Lake District, which she established in 1891, produced more exotic materials such as silk damask and samite (silk interwoven with silver thread). Katie Grasett opened the London School of Weaving in 1898, and here too silk damasks were woven, as well as brocades and other less sophisticated fabrics, usually in floral designs.

The Haslemere Peasant Industries established by Godfrey Blount

53

included hand-weaving among the crafts carried on. Edmund Hunter opened his St Edmundsbury Weaving Works in 1901, also at Haslemere, where he employed professional weavers from Spitalfields to make silk on jacquard looms. Luther Hooper, who was associated with Blount's enterprise, claimed in his book *Hand-Loom Weaving* published in 1910, that the jacquard loom had been responsible for the division between the designer and the weaver (the jacquard loom facilitates the weaving of very intricate patterns).

Hooper's book probably had some influence on Ethel Mairet who started hand-weaving at about this time. She had studied at first hand the crafts of spinning, dyeing and weaving as practised in Sri Lanka, and she produced silk, wool and cotton cloths (and weaves in various combinations of different yarns) pat-terned according to the structure of the weave. In 1916 *A Book on Vegetable Dyes* by Ethel Mairet was published by Douglas Pepler and printed at the Hampshire House Workshops.

Another weaver who dyed her own yarns was Jean Orage, who wove rugs and tapestries designed by Edward McKnight Kauffer, Marion Dorn and Ronald Grierson.

HAND-PRINTED FABRICS

Morris & Co. made hand-printed textiles with designs by William Morris and J.H. Dearle. For Wardle's of Leek, Walter Crane and Lewis F. Day, among others, designed printed textiles. The firm of Alexander

Morris & Co. printed cotton
***Tulip* curtain**
180 × 266cm
Haslam & Whiteway, London
Price (pair): £700

Embroidered and appliquéd
hanging by Anne Knox Arthur
62 × 62cm
Paul Reeves, London
Price: £450

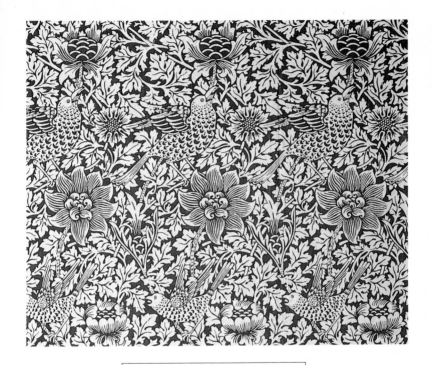

Morris & Co. printed cotton
Bird and Anemone
98 × 165cm
Paul Reeves, London
Price: £160

Morton & Co. of Darvel near Kilmarnock produced machine-woven textiles designed by Heywood Sumner of the Century Guild, Walton and Voysey, and block-printed linen designed by Jessie M. King (the furniture designer E.W. Taylor's wife). But these textiles, commissioned by firms and produced by industrial processes, are at best peripheral to the Arts and Crafts movement.

Mention should be made of the Crysède printed silks made at the Cornish fishing port of Newlyn during the 1920s. They were designed by Alec Walker who owned a silk mill in Yorkshire. At first the silk was processed in Yorkshire and then sent to Newlyn for printing, but later the raw silk was bleached, dyed and block-printed by hand in Newlyn. It was sold at a shop on the premises either by the yard or made up into garments. After meeting the French painter and textile designer Raoul Dufy, Walker adopted a more colourful, modern style of design which proved very popular.

Object	Quality of Manufacture	Quality of design and/or decoration	Rarity	Price (£)	Price ($)
Anon.					
Walnut/beech armchair	7	7	■■	250–500	440–875
Oak side table	7	7	■■	400–800	700–1400
Mahogany pot stand	7	8	■	250–400	440–700
Embroidered linen hanging	8	7	■■	400–700	700–1225
Birch, W.					
Oak armchair designed by E.G. Punnett	8	9	■■	700–1000	1225–1750
Broadwood & Sons					
Oak piano designed by M.H. Baillie Scott	8	8	■■	800–1000+	1400–1750+
Gimson, E.					
Oak ladderback chair	9	8	■■■	300–500	525–875
Walnut prie dieu	10	9	■■■	600–1000+	1050–1750+
Heal & Son					
Oak cabinet designed by A. Heal	9	9	■■	800–1000+	1400–1750+
Oak occasional table	9	8	■■	250–500	440–875
Oak dressing table	8	7	■	300–550	525–965
Holland & Sons					
Oak side chair designed by G.E. Street	8	9	■■■	500–800	875–1400
Kenton & Co.					
Mahogany shelves	8	7	■■■	450–750	790–1315
Liberty & Co.					
Oak side chair	7	7	■■	300–600	525–1050
Oak cabinet	7	7	■■	600–1000	1050–1750

Quality on a scale 1–10   ■ Rare   ■■ Very rare   ■■■ Extremely rare

Object	Quality of Manufacture	Quality of design and/or decoration	Rarity	Price (£)	Price ($)
Michigan Chair Co.					
Oak tabouret	7	7	■■	400–800	700–1400
Morris & Co.					
Mahogany table designed by G. Jack	8	9	■■■	950–1000+	1665–1750+
Rush-seated armchair designed by D.G. Rossetti	8	9	■■	300–500	525–875
Pair printed cotton curtains	8	9	■■	550–850	965–1490
Pugin, A.W.N.					
Oak side chair	8	9	■■■	600–1000	1050–1750
Roycroft					
Oak side chair	8	8	■■	800–1000+	1400–1750+
Russell, G.					
Cuban mahogany serving table	9	8	■■	700–1000	1225–1750
Stickley, G.					
Oak side chair	8	8	■■	350–900	615–1575
Oak desk	8	8	■■	700–1000	1225–1750
Oak tabouret	8	8	■■	400–800	790–1400
Oak ladderback chair	8	8	■■	525–600	615–1050
Oak rocking chair	8	8	■■	800–1000+	1400–1750+
Embroidered linen table scarf	8	8	■■■	700–1000	1225–1750
Stickley, L. & J.G.					
Oak table	7	8	■■	400–800	790–1400
Wylie & Lochhead					
Oak armchair	8	8	■■	600–1000	1050–1750
Mahogany cupboard	8	8	■■	750–1000+	1315–1750+

Quality on a scale 1–10   ■ Rare   ■■ Very rare   ■■■ Extremely rare

CHAPTER TWO

METALWORK

Keswick School of Industrial Art
silver teapot. Paul Reeves, London.
Price: £850

The spectrum of Arts and Crafts metalwork is wide. Through crudely hammered copper vases at one extreme, and finely planished silver cups at the other, artists and craftsmen endeavoured to express the beauty of their materials and the sincerity of their ideas. A variety of materials was used, including copper and other base metals, silver and silver plate, gold and enamels.

COPPER AND OTHER BASE METALS

Between 1881 and 1886 Philip Webb built the country house Clouds at East Knoyle, Wiltshire, for the Hon. Percy Wyndham. A few years after its completion, a fire damaged part of the house and the Wyndhams were forced to take refuge in the servants' quarters. Mrs Wyndham wrote to a friend: 'It is a good thing that our architect was a Socialist, because we find ourselves just as comfortable in the servants' quarters as we were in our own.' That the Wyndhams accepted the servants' quarters so easily is a testimony to the levelling instinct found among most Arts and Crafts architects and designers. Wherever there was an established scale of values, attempts were made to abolish the accepted distinctions and this included metals.

Before the Arts and Crafts movement, copper was confined below stairs. The metals permitted in sitting rooms and drawing rooms were gold, silver, plate, brass and perhaps bronze. But, like oak and stoneware, two other materials that had been relegated to the tavern or the servants' quarters, copper was favoured by the Arts and Crafts movement. It appealed to designers and craftsmen not only because of its humble rank but also because of its aesthetic merits. Copper has beautiful colour and texture and records the marks of the craftsman's tools clearly. It is very malleable and is one of the easiest metals to work. Moreover, it is an inexpensive metal, which helps to explain its lowly status prior to the Arts and Crafts movement. Its relative cheapness is also another reason for its attraction; amateur and semi-professional craftsmen do not like spending a lot on raw materials, particularly when sales are expected to be, at best, moderate. But it was to become even cheaper; in the United States production of copper rose from 12,500 tonnes in 1872 to 76,000 tonnes in 1885. The enormous increase in output led to a dramatic drop in price.

W.A.S. BENSON

Morris & Co. does not seem to have made any metal products, so it is not surprising that when the young W.A.S. Benson consulted William Morris about a career in the crafts he was steered towards metalwork (probably with a view to commissioning metalwork designs for Morris & Co.). Early in the 1880s Benson set up a workshop manufacturing domestic utensils in copper and brass. He then built a factory at the Eyot Works, St Peters Square, Hammersmith, and in 1887 opened a showroom at 82–83 New Bond Street. Benson is an anomaly in the Arts and Crafts movement. Although he was close to William Morris, and became chairman of the Firm on Morris's death in 1896, and although he adhered strongly to the Arts and Crafts ethic regarding design and materials, his methods of production were quite pragmatic. For example, he had no

Copper and isinglass table lamp
Height: 53.3cm
Sold: Phillips, New York, 27/6/87
Price: $660

scruples about using machines such as spinning lathes and a stamping plant, and made a speciality of electric-light fittings which the *Magazine of Art* described in 1896 as 'palpitatingly modern'.

REPOUSSÉ WORK IN ENGLAND

The two principal designers of the Century Guild, Arthur Heygate Mackmurdo and his partner Herbert Horne, designed objects in copper and brass. Candlesticks, light fittings, plaques, dishes and fenders were made in brass by George Esling, a member of the Guild; Kellock Brown, another member, executed designs for wall-sconces and panels in copper. These objects were sometimes pierced for decoration, but were more often repoussé (hammered into relief), a technique which became popular during the 1880s. Charles Godfrey Leland, an American who organized craft training for the poor in Philadelphia, wrote a series of *Art Work Manuals*, one of which, published in 1883, was *Repoussé Work or Embossing on Sheet Brass*.

Leland's activities inspired the foundation in Britain of the Home Arts and Industries Association, established in 1885 by Mrs Jebb of Ellesmere in Shropshire. With keen support from Mackmurdo, she set up training studios at Langham Place, London, and arranged courses up and down the country which offered instruction in various crafts. At that time there was a serious agricultural recession and many labourers had been thrown off the land. Mrs Jebb's notion was to provide them with a stimulating and improving, if not particularly lucrative, occupation. The Association, which organized regular exhibitions at the Albert Hall

W.A.S. Benson copper and brass kettle on iron stand
Height: 78.5cm
Sold: Sotheby's, London, 19/12/86
Price: £638

**W.A.S. Benson copper and brass
kettle and muffin-dish on stand**
Height: 99.2cm
Haslam & Whiteway, London
Price: £1000

**W.A.S. Benson copper
and brass candlestick**
Length: 29.7cm
Paul Reeves, London
Price: £380

in London, was responsible for much of the repoussé decorated copper and brass that is so plentiful in Britain today.

Following the lead set by the Home Arts and Industries Association, various institutions began to produce similar work in copper and brass. The Keswick School of Industrial Art, which had been established by Canon Rawnsley in 1884, started making copper vases, trays, jugs and other items, decorated with repoussé and chased ornament. In 1898 the designer Harold Stabler was put in charge, and the School's metalwork assumed a more sophisticated style.

Another enterprise which reflected the vogue for repoussé copper and brass was C.R. Ashbee's Guild of Handicraft, founded in 1888 at Whitechapel, London. The metalwork produced during the first few years of the Guild was nearly all of this sort. The principal craftsman was John Pearson who had previously been employed at William de Morgan's tile works. At the Guild, he created a decorative style based loosely on motifs used by De Morgan, for example sea-serpents, peacocks, galleons and stylized flowers.

In 1892 Ashbee took Pearson to task for supplying other organizations with ornamental metalwork, and as a result Pearson resigned from the Guild of Handicraft and went to Cornwall where he imparted his skills to the Newlyn Industrial Class, founded in 1890 by the painter John D. Mackenzie. Over the next forty years this enterprise produced

Keswick School of Industrial Art
copper tray
Length: 71.4cm
Haslam & Whiteway, London
Price: £320

**Copper jardinière
on wrought-iron stand**
Height: 107.5cm
Sold: Sotheby's, London, 19/12/86
Price: £660

Copper wall-sconce by John Pearson
Height: 35.8cm
Paul Reeves, London
Price: £125

enormous quantities of utility wares in copper and other base metals with repoussé decoration, most of which was designed by Mackenzie. The same sort of wares were produced by the Yattendon Metalworking Class; this was started in 1890 by Elizabeth Waterhouse (the wife of the architect Alfred Waterhouse), at Yattendon, Berkshire. Repoussé decorated metalwork was shown by both the Newlyn and Yattendon classes at the exhibitions organized by the Home Arts and Industries Association at the Albert Hall in London.

The Barnstaple Metalworkers' Guild, founded by G. Lloyd Morris around 1900, and the classes at Newton, Cambridgeshire, and Fivemiletown, County Tyrone in Ireland, (both run for a time by John Williams, previously one of Pearson's colleagues at the Guild of Handicraft), all produced more of the same sort of repoussé-decorated copper and brass.

Richard Llewellyn Rathbone, a relation of W.A.S. Benson (whose example may well have influenced his choice of career), set up as a metalworker in the early 1890s. In 1893 he provided gas fittings for a hotel in Cheshire designed by Mackmurdo, and in 1897 he made decorative metalwork for a London church designed by Heywood Sumner. He also made copper and brass utensils from designs by C.F.A. Voysey. From 1898 to 1903 he taught a metalwork class at the University of Liverpool and opened his own workshop, where he was assisted by Harold Stabler. Then he came to London where he opened another workshop. He made a wide range of utility wares in hammered copper and brass, with very restrained decoration which was either embossed or punched.

THE GLASGOW SCHOOL

Some metalwork in the style which evolved at the Glasgow School of Art under Francis Newbery can be found with repoussé decoration. In 1893, two of the School's ex-pupils, the sisters Margaret and Mary Gilmour, established a studio in West George Street, Glasgow, where they taught a variety of crafts. Margaret Gilmour was an accomplished metalworker, making items such as sconces, candlesticks and mirror frames in brass and other base metals decorated with repoussé designs of, for example, peacocks or formalized roses.

Copper candlestick
Height: 19.6cm
Haslam & Whiteway, London
Price (pair): £320

67

Another pair of sisters, Margaret and Frances Macdonald, also studied at the Glasgow School of Art. From the mid-1890s they sometimes collaborated on objects made of hammered copper, brass or tin, repoussé decorated with motifs characteristics of the Glasgow style. Frances Macdonald also produced such objects on her own. From 1907 she gave instruction in metalwork at the Glasgow School of Art.

Talwin Morris, art director of Blackie & Sons the Glasgow publishers, designed metalwork including copper mirror frames which were decorated with repoussé ornament, often with a distinctive heart-shaped motif.

LIBERTY & CO.

When Liberty & Co. launched a range of pewter ware in 1903, the company commissioned designs from several artists associated with the Arts and Crafts movement. One of the strongest influences on the design of 'Tudric' pewter, as Liberty's christened their new line, was the Glasgow style, particularly those elements of it that were derived from ancient Celtic ornament. Such artists as Bernard Cuzner, a Birmingham metalworker, sold designs to Liberty & Co. The firm often modified designs in order to make the objects easier to produce in quantity; elements from different designs were sometimes combined in a single object. But a place in the Arts and Crafts movement can scarcely be claimed for Liberty's pewter since it was manufactured at the Birmingham works of W.H. Haseler, using essentially industrial mass-production processes. All the pewter was cast in iron moulds.

Gordon Russell steel fire-irons
Height: 59.3cm
Paul Reeves, London
Price: £450

**Silver-plated soup spoon
designed by C.R. Mackintosh**
Length: 18.5cm
Sold: Phillips, London, 18/6/87
Price (with a smaller, similar spoon):
£110

FORGED METALWORK

Around 1905, Ernest Gimson took on a young blacksmith called Alfred Bucknell to make strap hinges and handles for his furniture. Bucknell worked mainly in steel, forging such items as firedogs, trivets, candlesticks and candelabra to Gimson's designs, as well as furniture fittings. He usually sherardized his work, a process which includes coating the steel with zinc by heating it in contact with zinc dust. Bucknell also made brass pitchers and bowls, and copper sconces. Decoration was restrained and simple, usually consisting of chased floral ornament.

While the art of the blacksmith was being revived by Gimson and Bucknell in Gloucestershire, the jeweller and metalworker Nelson Dawson and the designer Edward Spencer were performing the same task in London. In 1901 they had started the Artificers' Guild with workshops in Oil Mill Lane, Chiswick, where a wide range of metalwork was made. Dawson combined forged iron with silver or brass, and Spencer designed a range of items in wrought iron, including firedogs, candlesticks and sconces. The Artificers' Guild also made articles of copper and bronze, sometimes mounted with silver, and most of them designed by Edward Spencer. Both artists used the services of the blacksmith Walter Spencer (no relation). Edward and Walter Spencer published two articles, both entitled 'Wrought Iron Work', one of which appeared in the *Art Journal* in 1908 and the other in an edition of *Studio* in 1909.

Some established firms of metalwork manufacturers made items designed by prominent figures in the Arts and Crafts movement. For example, Longden & Co. made steel firedogs designed by George Jack, and firedogs and candlesticks designed by W.R. Lethaby. Thomas Elsley's Portland Metal Works made an iron fire-grate by Lethaby, and bronze table lamps by C.F.A. Voysey. The Falkland Iron Company produced cast iron fireplaces designed by Ashbee and Benson, and the Coalbrookdale Company made them to designs by Benson and Lethaby.

DRYAD METALWORK

In 1912, the Dryad Works, established at Leicester five years earlier to make cane furniture, merged with the firm of Collins & Co., also of Leicester, which produced art metalwork. The new enterprise was called' Dryad Metal Works and, like the cane furniture workshop, used designs supplied by teachers at the Leicester School of Art. One of them was John Sidney Reeve who taught silversmithing and metalwork and who had previously been a member of Ashbee's Guild of Handicraft.

Dryad Metal Works produced door furniture, candlesticks, bowls and other items in bronze and hot-water jugs in copper, as well as silver and jewellery. The objects have virtually no ornament, relying for their decorative effect on form and finish instead. Gordon Russell's furniture workshops at Broadway in Worcestershire produced a limited amount of items in brass and steel in the early 1920s, usually decorated with punched or chased ornament.

METALWORKING IN AMERICA

In America, Arts and Crafts metalwork does not seem to have been produced until the late 1890s. Leland's manuals did not apparently inspire the amateur craftsmen in his

Candleholder by E.T.O. Fish
Height: 22.5cm
Michael Carey Inc., New York
Price: $250

Copper tray
Length: 32.8cm
Michael Carey Inc., New York
Price: $600

Bronze candelabra by
E.T. Hurley
Height: 32.5cm
Michael Carey Inc., New York
Price: $1250

own land the way they did in England. But it may also have been that the industrial production of art metalwork by firms such as Gorham and Tiffany absorbed all the available talent at that time.

One of the first American Arts and Crafts metalworkers was Madeline Yale Wynne, the daughter of Linus Yale Jr, the inventor of the Yale lock. From an early age she had 'access to shop and machinery', as she recalled in 1906. She 'thus naturally became interested in Arts and Crafts' and claimed to have 'developed my own line in metalwork and enamels without instruction'. She taught drawing for several years at the School of the Museum of Fine Arts in Boston, and when she moved to Chicago, in about 1894, established a studio in the Tree Building where she was soon making metalwork and jewellery. In 1897 she was one of the founders of the Chicago Arts and Crafts Society, and she regularly showed her work at its exhibitions. She made small items in coarsely hammered copper, often set with natural pebbles. 'I consider', she wrote, 'each effort by itself as regards colour and form much as I would paint a picture.'

At the third exhibition of the Chicago Arts and Crafts Society, held in 1900, lanterns and candlesticks designed and made by Robert Riddle

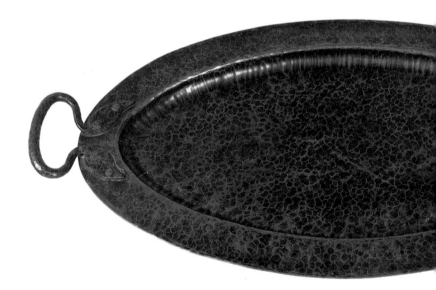

Gustav Stickley copper tray
Length: 60cm
Sold: Phillips, New York, 27/6/87
Price: $550

Jarvie first attracted general attention. Jarvie was a clerk in Chicago's city administration who had taken up metalwork as a hobby. Such was the success of his candlesticks, which were cast in bronze or copper, brush polished and sometimes patinated, that he abandoned his career in municipal government and opened The Jarvie Shop. By 1906 Jarvie had retail outlets in more than ten states. His candlesticks are tall, slender, flower-like forms which owe something to Tiffany's lampstands but are plainer and more classical in feeling.

In 1903 Gustav Stickley began importing English Arts and Crafts metalwork which he marketed under

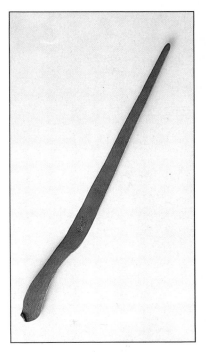

**Gustav Stickley copper
paper-knife**
Length: 22.8cm
Michael Carey Inc., New York
Price: $850

the Craftsman banner. Soon, however, copper ware was being manufactured at his workshops in Eastwood, New York. Repoussé wall plaques and an extensive range of utility items appeared in the Craftsman catalogues. Stickley's metalwork had a simplicity bordering on austerity, relieved only by the richness of the materials used and the fine craftsmanship. In the last few years of Stickley's venture, before he went bankrupt in 1915, his copper was usually given an artificial patina.

73

Elbert Hubbard, too, noted the growing demand for Arts and Crafts metalwork and decided to add 'art copper' to the books, tooled leather, sculpture and furniture already being produced at the Roycroft workshops in East Aurora. In 1909 Hubbard asked Karl Kipp, a former banker who had arrived at Roycroft the year before and was working in the bindery, to establish a copper workshop. Kipp designed each item and a prototype was passed to an assistant who made the tools suitable for its manufacture. Many of the designs incorporated repoussé ornament, for example a bookend decorated with a poppy motif. Among other items produced were smoker's sets, inkwells, trays, and candlesticks.

**Roycroft copper candlesticks
designed by Karl Kipp**
Height: 19.2cm
Sold: Phillips, New York, 27/6/87
Price: $605

Roycroft copper smoker's stand
Height: 75cm
Sold: Phillips, New York, 27/6/87
Price: $880

Kipp also made stands and shades for leaded glass lamps designed by Dard Hunter, who had been at Roycroft since 1903. Hunter's style was influenced by illustrations that he had seen of contemporary German and Austrian decorative art. In 1908 he took a trip to Vienna and on his return many of his designs showed characteristics of the Wiener Werkstätte style created by Josef Hoffman, Kolo Moser and Otto Prutscher. Some of this rubbed off on Kipp, and much of the copper ware that he produced has a Viennese look.

In 1911 Karl Kipp left Roycroft and set up his own workshop in East Aurora, called The Tookay Shop ('two K'). His departure may well have been due to some personal difference with Elbert Hubbard because, on the latter's death in 1915, he returned to Roycroft.

Around 1905, Newcomb College in New Orleans, Louisiana, added metalwork to its production of pottery. At first, brass shades were made for ceramic lampstands. The brass was shaped by hammering it over a wooden form, and was then pierced with small openings arranged in decorative patterns. Subsequently the same process was used to make items in copper, such as bookends. Hammered copper bowls were also produced at the College.

Roycroft copper bookends
Height: 10.1cm
Michael Carey Inc., New York
Price: $750

Roycroft copper candlesticks
Height: 30.8cm
Michael Carey Inc., New York
Price: $800

In Oakland, California, a Dutch immigrant called Dirk Van Erp opened a metal workshop in 1908. As a coppersmith working in the San Francisco shipyards, Van Erp had made decorative vases from brass shell-casings, as a sideline. In 1910 he established a workshop at 1104 Sutter Street, San Francisco, with Eleanor D'Arcy Gaw from Montreal, who had trained at the Art Institute in Chicago and with Ashbee's Guild of Handicraft. It was a successful partnership but lasted only about a year. Miss Gaw provided designs for a range of items, particularly lamps and vases, which Van Erp made in hammered copper.

Birmingham Guild of Handicraft copper lamp
Height: 55.8cm
Paul Reeves, London
Price: £950

Copper vase by Dirk Van Erp
Height: 15.3cm
Michael Carey Inc., New York
Price: $1500

After Miss Gaw's departure, Van Erp remained at Sutter Street and made objects such as lamps, desk sets and trays, designed by himself and various other artists including Thomas McGlynn, who had earlier assisted Arthur Mathews at the Furniture Shop. Van Erp's copper ware is notable for the graceful simplicity of its forms, sometimes inspired by oriental design, together with the high quality of the craftsmanship.

Silver dish by Gilbert Marks
Diameter: 22cm
Sold: Sotheby's, London, 16/5/86
Price: £462

Harry St John Dixon, who had trained in Van Erp's workshop, opened his own workshops in San Francisco after the First World War and made a range of copper ware that was similar to Van Erp's output. His brother, the painter Maynard Dixon, had a formative influence on the style of Harry's designs.

The Handicraft Guild of Minneapolis, founded in 1902 by Ernest A. Batchelder as a craft school rather than a workshop, sold its members' work as far afield as New York and Philadelphia. The metalwork made by the Guild included copper items such as boxes and bowls, usually decorated with repoussé work and sometimes set with semi-precious stones.

SILVERWORK IN BRITAIN

Articles in silver tend to be more expensive than other Arts and Crafts metalwork (except for gold) simply because of the greater intrinsic value of the material. During the last quarter of the nineteenth century, the difference in price between silver and base metals was roughly as great as it is today, despite the steady fall in the value of silver; between 1873, when it was worth 5s. an ounce (as it had been for decades), and 1888, it dropped by more than 25 per cent to 3s. 7d. an ounce. The slide was the result of increased production, particularly in the USA and Australia. The gold standard, meanwhile, was becoming increasingly recognized among the important trading nations. The value of gold fluctuated so little that the Chambers Encyclopaedia of 1890 could blandly state: 'Pure gold (24 carat) is worth £4, 4s. 11½d. per oz.' In comparison with gold, silver assumed the character of a poor relation, which inevitably enhanced its appeal to the metalworkers of the Arts and Crafts movement.

The earliest Arts and Crafts silversmith in Britain was Gilbert Leigh Marks. He worked for a firm of manufacturing silversmiths from 1878 to 1885, when he set up his own workshop. There he insisted on doing everything by hand, but his work still retained a professional look which almost debars it from being classified as Arts and Crafts. He usually decorated his work with repoussé floral designs which, however, are more reminiscent of the precise realism attained by industrial silversmiths than the broadly handled fantasy characteristic of John Pearson's work produced at the Guild of Handicraft. Occasionally, Marks worked in pewter.

Some of the metalwork produced by W.A.S. Benson was silver-plated, but he seems to have made few articles in solid silver. The same can be said of the Keswick School of Industrial Art. The Birmingham Guild of Handicraft, however, seems to have produced almost as much work in silver as in copper. The Birmingham Guild was started about 1890 as an evening class run by Arthur Stansfield Dixon, who designed much of the silverware produced. In 1895 the Guild became a limited company and later moved from its original premises in Kyrle Hall to workshops at 45 Great Charles Street, Birmingham, designed by Dixon. Domestic and ecclesiastical silver was made by the Guild, and their coffee pots and jugs, particularly, are notable for their clean lines and lack of any ornament; the hammered finish is only lightly planished. Dixon was friendly with William Morris, and Birmingham Guild metalwork was sold at Morris & Co. in Oxford Street, London.

**Guild of Handicraft silver
porringer designed by
C.R. Ashbee**
Length: 15cm
Paul Reeves, London
Price: £850

Ashbee regarded silverware as 'that most degraded of all English crafts' and with his usual missionary zeal set about reforming it. By 1895 his Guild of Handicraft was producing silver cups and presentation spoons, and the range was subsequently expanded to include a wide variety of domestic silver. Production was increased when the Guild moved in 1902 to Chipping Campden in the Cotswolds. A characteristic of the Guild's silver is the use of wirework for handles and finials, and many pieces were set with semi-precious stones. The principal silversmiths were William Hardiman, James Baily and George Hart. After the Guild's liquidation in 1907, Hart and Baily continued making silver at Chipping Campden in the style that C.R. Ashbee had originally conceived.

When architect J.D. Sedding died unexpectedly in 1891, his practice was carried on by his chief assistant Henry Wilson. He finished a number of commissions outstanding at Sedding's death but he turned more and more to metalwork and jewellery. Most of his silver was ecclesiastical;

Guild of Handicraft silver tray
Length: 64cm
Sold: Phillips, London, 24/3/87
Price: £902

Guild of Handicraft silver salts
Height: 6.5cm
Sold: Sotheby's, London, 4/6/87
Price: £528

he did, however, make a few domestic pieces, and occasionally worked in pewter. His style was derived from English medieval metalwork and Byzantine architectural forms. He was the author of *Silverwork and Jewellery*, published in 1903.

John Paul Cooper, who had been articled to Sedding, continued his training under Wilson, on whose advice he too took up metalwork and jewellery. From 1904 to 1907 he taught at the Birmingham School of Art, and he then built himself a house and workshop at Westerham, Kent. His style was always close to Wilson's. He often used natural materials in conjunction with silver, for instance coconut shell, abalone, ostrich-egg shell and narwhal tusk, and

he revived the art of working in shagreen, a type of finely granulated leather. His wooden boxes covered with pieces of shagreen are mounted with decorated strips of silver which hide the seams.

The sculptor Louis Richard Garbe, a member of the Guild of Art Craftsmen, also made objects covered with shagreen, although they were mounted with brass and wrought iron rather than silver.

**Enamelled copper vase
by Hubert von Herkomer**
Height: 24.5cm
Sold: Phillips, London, 18/6/87
Price: £605

Cooper generally executed his designs himself, but he also designed for the Artificers' Guild. Nelson Dawson, who founded the Guild with Edward Spencer, had in 1897 made an iron and brass screen at the church of the Holy Trinity in Sloane Street, London, one of the buildings Sedding left unfinished at his death. The screen was designed by Henry Wilson. From 1899 Wilson's silver was sold at a gallery in Maddox Street, London, belonging to Montague Fordham who had previously been a director of the Birmingham Guild of Handicraft. When Nelson Dawson left the Artificers' Guild in 1903, Montague Fordham took it over. So it is not altogether surprising to find Cooper designing for the Guild, and it is quite understandable that much of the silver and plate that Spencer designed is in a style related to that of Wilson and Cooper.

Omar Ramsden started his career in a Sheffield silversmith's workshop, attending evening classes at the local art school. He became friendly with a fellow-student, Alwyn Carr, and in 1896 they both won scholarships to the National Art Training School at South Kensington, London (now the Royal College of Art). In 1898 they set up a partnership, producing a wide range of gold and silverware, from napkin rings to elaborate ceremonial pieces. Although the style of their work is related to the Arts and Crafts movement, there are often strong elements of Continental Art Nouveau in their design and decoration. Their industrial background gives some of their pieces a look of slick professionalism which is alien to the Arts and Crafts philosophy.

The Duchess of Sutherland's Cripples Guild produced silverware with chased and repoussé decoration

which was sold at their premises in Bond Street, London. Much of it was in the style of seventeenth-century English silver. The Guild also made articles in copper and plate.

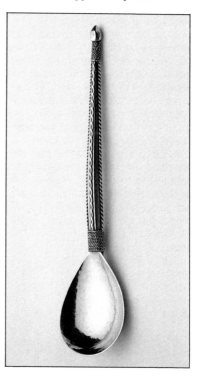

**Artificers' Guild silver spoon
designed by Edward Spencer**
Length: 15.1cm
Paul Reeves, London
Price: £250

The Birmingham firm of Haseler's also made silverware for Liberty & Co. as well as pewter. Although at first a few pieces were made entirely by hand, spinning lathes, hand-operated presses and foot-operated drop stamps were generally used. The design of each object was scrutinized at the factory to work out the most economical means of manufacturing it. It was called 'Cymric', and most of the designers were those who later worked on the 'Tudric' line in pewter. One of them was the Birmingham silversmith and metalworker Bernard Cuzner. His own silverwork was in a more traditional style, decorated with repoussé, embossed or chased ornament and sometimes set with semi-precious stones. Cuzner also worked in base metals, particularly brass.

A. Edward Jones, also a Birmingham designer, and the son of a blacksmith, expanded the family business to include silversmithing. The firm was producing silverware from 1902, most of it in a style close to the Birmingham Guild of Handicraft, some of whose members probably supplied designs. It is often set with turquoise. Jones sometimes made silver mounts for pieces of William Howson Taylor's pottery. The two men were good friends.

SILVERWORK IN CHICAGO

Madeline Yale Wynne worked in silver as well as base metals, and taught silversmithing skills to other Chicago ladies, including Mrs Homer Taylor and Mrs Frances Glessner. The latter, whose husband John Glessner had commissioned pieces of furniture from Isaac Scott during the 1870s, had the conservatory of 1800 Prairie Avenue (the Glessner home) converted into a workshop where she made her silverware.

In 1905, George S. Welles, a Chicago businessman with interests in coal and also an amateur metalworker, married Clara Pauline Barck who had attended design classes at the Art Institute of Chicago and ran the Kalo Shop where she made and sold burnt-leather wares and simple jewellery. Together they started the Kalo Art-Craft Community at their home in Park Ridge, a suburb of Chicago. Mrs Welles hired professional silversmiths who made articles to her designs, and soon cutlery and other domestic items in hand-beaten silver constituted the bulk of what was sold at the Kalo Shop. The designs often show the influence of Guild of Handicraft silverware (Ashbee had visited Chicago and had lectured at the Art Institute in 1900, the year Mrs Welles had been a student there). Kalo Shop silverware is occasionally set with semi-precious stones or jade, but generally relies for its decorative effect on an applied monogram and the texture of its hammered finish.

Around 1910 Robert Riddle Jarvie turned his attention from cast brass or copper candlesticks to handbeaten silverware. At the same time his style became more architectonic, which was probably due to his friendship with the architect George Grant Elmslie. Occasionally Elmslie provided Jarvie with designs for silverware. Like Kalo Shop silver, Jarvie's work was often decorated with an applied monogram. Arthur G. Leonard, president of the Union Stockyard Company, admired Jarvie's silver and asked him to make several trophies which were awarded to champion cattle breeders.

SILVERWORK IN BOSTON

The Handicraft Shop at Boston was founded in 1901 under the auspices of the city's Society of Arts and Crafts. Arthur Astor Carey, president

**Guild of Handicraft silver-
plated and chalcedony epergne**
Height: 27.5cm
Sold: Phillips, London, 18/6/87
Price: £682

of the Society, provided the finance, and Mary Catherine Knight, who had been a designer with the Gorham Manufacturing Company, was appointed to supervise the workshops. By 1906 the Shop was producing silverware and metalwork. Miss Knight collaborated with professional silversmiths, notably Karl F. Leinonen, producing articles in a style derived from silver of the American colonial era. Between 1903 and 1907 the Handicraft Shop was moved to Wellesley Hills in rural Massachusetts, in emulation of the Guild of Handicraft's exodus from London to the Cotswolds. However, the new location was found unsatisfactory, and the shop very soon returned to Boston.

Two other important Boston silversmiths were immigrants who had learnt the craft in their native lands: Arthur J. Stone and George Ernest Germer. Stone had worked for a master-silversmith in Sheffield, England, attending art school in the evenings in much the same way and in the same city as Omar Ramsden was to do some thirty years later. Stone sailed to the USA in 1884 and settled three years later in Gardner, Massachusetts. From 1904 he won a succession of important commissions from members of the Boston Society of Arts and Crafts. He worked in silver and copper, and his pieces are well designed and superbly crafted. Ornament, which he used sparingly, consists of flora and fauna modelled naturalistically.

Germer had been apprenticed to a silversmith as a boy in Berlin. He came to America in 1893 and for twenty years worked as a designer, modeller and chaser for leading silverware manufacturers in Boston, Providence, Rhode Island, and New York. In 1912 he joined the Boston Society of Arts and Crafts and began making ecclesiastical silver, usually decorated with Gothic ornament modelled in high relief.

OTHER SILVERWORK SCHOOLS IN AMERICA

Theodore Hanford Pond ran the Pond Applied Art Studios at Baltimore, Maryland, from 1911 to 1914. Earlier he had worked for Tiffany, designing stained glass, and he had taught at the Rhode Island School of Design. His silver is simple but satisfying, reticently decorated with chased and repoussé ornament.

Clemens Friedell, another silversmith, was born in New Orleans, but he went at an early age with his parents to their native Vienna, where he was apprenticed to a silversmith for seven years. Returning to America in 1892 he worked for a jeweller in San Antonio, Texas, until 1901 when he took a job with the Gorham Manufacturing Company. He was laid off in 1907 and two years later went to Pasadena, California. There he set up his own workshop and made hand-beaten silver tableware and trophies often decorated with motifs drawn from the flora of California.

Finally, there are the extraordinary creations of Janet Payne Bowles. In 1899 she moved from Indianapolis to Boston where her husband Joseph M. Bowles transferred the offices of his periodical *Modern Art*. She studied psychology under William James at Radcliffe and took part in some activities of the Society of Arts and Crafts. She learnt the basic techniques of metalwork from a Russian immigrant and in 1907, having moved to New York, set up her own workshop on 28th Street. She soon

85

**Guild of Handicraft silver and
enamel bowl and cover**
Height: 9.7cm
Paul Reeves, London
Price: £550

started winning prizes for her silver which became increasingly unorthodox; although it contains references to a wide variety of historical styles, it seems to express vividly the soul of its maker. It often combines many different techniques, for example hammering, bending, cutting, curling, soldering and raising. 'Janet Payne Bowles seeks to express', wrote a critic in *International Studio* in 1923, 'the universal and eternal in rhythmic modelling of gold and silver'.

ENAMELS

Three kinds of enamelling were widely used by Arts and Crafts metalworkers. The *cloisonné* technique, where the different colours of the design are kept apart by thin metal strips laid on the area being decorated, was revived during the second half of the nineteenth century in response to the vogue for all things Japanese. The *champlevé* technique is similar, but the compartments for the different colours are formed by depressions made in the metal surface, which is then decorated. Among Arts and Crafts metalworkers *cloisonné* and *champlevé* enamelling was more general in the United States than in Britain, especially after the Limoges technique was made accessible to British craftsmen. Using the Limoges method, it is possible to gradate the colours and achieve a much more painterly effect. It is a more difficult process, requiring very delicate brushwork and a great number of firings. The attraction of enamelling to artist-craftsmen, apart from its aesthetic qualities, was that it did not need particularly sophisticated equipment.

BRITISH ENAMELWORKERS

In 1882 the painter James Tissot included more than twenty *cloisonné* enamelled items, which he had made, in an exhibition of his work at the Dudley Gallery in Piccadilly, London. They showed considerable Oriental influence and were not far removed, either in style or technique, from the *cloisonné* enamelled wares that had been produced by the great metalwork manufacturers Barbedienne and Christofle in France, and Elkington in Britain. What aroused the admiration of the critics was that an artist working without the resources of one of these large firms could bring off such a technical *tour de force*.

Tissot's enamels must also have enthused the young Clement Heaton whose father ran a firm of stained-glass manufacturers. Heaton, who was associated with the Century Guild, started making *cloisonné* enamels, some to designs by Mackmur-

**Silver and enamel bowl
by Harold Stabler**
Height: 6.6cm
Haslam & Whiteway, London
Price: £400

do, and he set up his own firm called Heaton's Cloisonné Mosaics Ltd. In the early 1890s he went to Switzerland and from there, in 1912, to the United States.

While studying art at the South Kensington schools, Alexander Fisher attended a lecture given by a French enameller. Fascinated by the subject, in 1884 he went to Paris to study the various techniques. On his return he set up a workshop and began making large and elaborate enamels using mainly the Limoges technique but also *cloisonné*, and sometimes both on the same piece. He taught enamelling at the Finsbury Technical College and the Central School of Arts and Crafts. He also took private pupils, one of whom was Nelson Dawson. Dawson taught the techniques to his wife, Edith, and together they produced articles in silver, brass, copper and iron decorated with enamels. Nelson designed the objects in his studio and Edith applied the enamels in what a contemporary writer called her 'artistic laboratory'.

In the early 1890s Constance Blount, wife of the poet and weaver Godfrey Blount, started making enamels. It may have been she who roused the enthusiasm of the painter Hubert von Herkomer who ran an art school which Godfrey Blount had attended. Herkomer's enamels were painted in the Limoges technique.

Constance Blount was consulted by Ashbee when he wanted to decorate Guild of Handicraft metalwork with enamels. Some of the Guild's craftsmen became proficient enamellers, particularly Fleetwood C. Varley who specialized in twilit landscapes. After the liquidation of the Guild, Varley painted enamel decorations on boxes made by Liberty & Co.

ENAMELLING IN SCOTLAND

Enamelling was one of the crafts practised by the artist-craftsmen of Glasgow. Dorothy Carleton-Smyth and De Courcy Lewthwaite Dewar (who taught metalwork and enamelling at the Glasgow School of Art for many years) both made silver articles in the Glasgow style decorated with enamels in the Limoges technique. Phoebe Traquair, who lived in Edinburgh, also made enamels, some of them very much in the style of Alexander Fisher.

AMERICAN ENAMELS

One of Fisher's pupils was the American artist Wilhelmina Stephan, who worked in collaboration with the Cleveland silversmith Horace E. Potter who had studied at the Guild of Handicraft in England. Their work shows the influence of the British Arts and Crafts movement.

Many of the more significant American enamellers were taught by Laurin H. Martin at the Cowles Art School in Boston. He too had been trained in England, but whether by Fisher or someone else does not seem to be known. Among his pupils were Mildred Watkins, another of a group of accomplished silversmiths working in Cleveland, and Elizabeth Copeland, who in 1904, after a short period working at the Handicraft Shop, set up her own workshop in Boston. Another of Martin's pupils was Douglas Donaldson who went to California and worked for a time at Batchelder's school of design and handicraft on the Arroyo Seco in Pasadena. He made items in silver and copper, often set with semi-precious stones and decorated with *champlevé* enamels.

**Silver and enamel cup and cover
by Nelson Dawson**
Height: 21.5cm
Sold: Sotheby's, London, 19/12/86
Price: £550

Object	Quality of manufacture	Quality of design and/or decoration	Rarity	Price (£)	Price ($)
Anon.					
Copper jardinière/iron stand	8	8	■■	400–800	700–1400
Copper repoussé tray	7	7	■	100–300	175–525
Copper and isinglass table lamp	8	8	■■	300–600	525–1050
Copper candlestick	7	7	■	50–150	90–265
Artificers' Guild					
Silver spoon	9	9	■■	200–400	350–700
Benson, W.A.S.					
Copper and brass kettle on stand	7	8	■■	600–1000+	1050–1750+
Copper and brass candlestick	7	8	■■	300–500	525–875
Birmingham Guild of Handicraft					
Copper table lamp	8	9	■■■	900–1000+	1575–1750+
Silver jug	8	9	■■■	750–1000+	1315–1750+
Century Guild					
Copper wall-sconce	8	9	■■■	600–900	1050–1575
Brass fender	8	9	■■■	800–1000+	1400–1750+
Clewell					
Metal-mounted ceramic vase	7	7	■■■	600–1000	1050–1750
Dawson, N.					
Silver and enamel cup and cover	8	9	■■■	500–800	875–1400
Dryad Metal Works					
Bronze candlesticks (pair)	9	8	■■■	100–200	175–350
Fish, E.T.O.					
Candleholder	8	8	■■■	150–250	265–440

Quality on a scale 1–10   ■ Rare   ■■ Very rare   ■■■ Extremely rare

Object	Quality of manufacture	Quality of design and/or decoration	Rarity	Price (£)	Price ($)
Germer, G.					
Silver bowl	9	8	■■■	800–1000+	1400–1750+
Gilmour, M.					
Copper/brass wall-sconce	8	8	■■■	500–1000+	875–1750+
Guild of Handicraft					
Silver tray	8	8	■■	850–1000+	1490–1750+
Silver-plated epergne	8	8	■■	650–950	1140–1665
Silver and enamel bowl and cover	8	8	■■	400–800	700–1400
Silver porringer	8	8	■■	500–1000+	875–1750+
Jarvie, R.					
Bronze/copper candlesticks (pair)	9	9	■■■	600–1000+	525–1750+
Kalo Shops					
Silver serving spoon	8	8	■■	75–150	135–265
Keswick School of Industrial Art					
Copper repoussé vase	8	8	■	50–150	90–265
Silver teapot	8	8	■■■	800–1000	1400–1750
Copper tray	8	8	■■	200–400	350–700
Mackintosh, C.R.					
Silver-plated soup spoon	7	9	■■	50–150	90–265
Marks, G.					
Silver dish	9	7	■■■	450–750	790–1315
Morris, T.					
Copper mirror frame	8	8	■■■	350–700	615–1225

Quality on a scale 1–10   ■ Rare   ■■ Very rare   ■■■ Extremely rare

Object	Quality of manufacture	Quality of design and/or decoration	Rarity	Price (£)	Price ($)
Newlyn Industrial Class					
Copper candlestick	7	8	■	40–80	70–140
Copper tray	7	8	■	60–120	105–210
Copper/brass wall-sconce	7	8	■	75–150	135–265
Copper and enamel box	8	8	■■■	120–240	210–420
Pearson, J.					
Copper repoussé wall-sconce	7	8	■■	75–150	135–265
Rathbone, R.					
Copper candlesticks (pair)	9	9	■■■	300–600	525–1050
Brass inkwell designed by C. Voysey	9	9	■■■	400–800	700–1400
Roycroft					
Pair copper candlesticks	8	8	■■	400–650	700–1140
Pair copper bookends	8	8	■■	400–600	700–1050
Copper smoker's stand	8	8	■■	600–900	1050–1575
Russell, G.					
Brass bowl	8	8	■■	150–300	265–525
Steel fire-irons	9	8	■■■	400–600	700–1050
Stabler, H.					
Silver and enamel bowl	8	8	■■■	350–500	615–875
Stickley, G.					
Copper paper-knife	8	8	■■■	400–700	700–1225
Copper tray	8	8	■■	350–600	615–1050
Tookay Shop					
Copper tray	8	8	■■■	300–600	525–1050

Quality on a scale 1–10   ■ Rare   ■■ Very rare   ■■■ Extremely rare

Object	Quality of manufacture	Quality of design and/or decoration	Rarity	Price (£)	Price ($)
Van Erp, D. Copper vase	9	8	■■	750–1000+	1315–1750+

Quality on a scale 1–10   ■ Rare   ■■ Very rare   ■■■ Extremely rare

CHAPTER THREE

CERAMICS

**Bernard Moore bowl decorated by Hilda
Beardmore. Richard Dennis, London.
Price: £350**

'I hope to find when I come back,' declared William de Morgan, writing from Italy to his partner in England, 'a mine of pots that might be Greek, Sicilian, Etruscan, Moorish, Italian Renaissance – anything but Staffordshire.' De Morgan's wish was in reaction to the state of the ceramics industry in Britain in the last quarter of the nineteenth century, which had grown to epitomize all that the idealists of the Arts and Crafts movement most despised. Quality had been sacrificed to profit.

Wherever possible, the machine had displaced the craftsman, the actions of the human hand had been made virtually automatic, and inferior materials were used because they were more amenable to mechanical production. Charles Fergus Binns, who worked at the Worcester porcelain factory until he was forty years old, and became the first director of the New York School of Clayworking and Ceramics, at Alfred, in 1898 wrote: 'The tendency of machine work has been to lower by small degrees the quality of the average earthenware body, as well as to rob the art of the potter of all its poetry and romance.' He described the soulless work of a china decorator: 'He has painted these flowers so often that their forms are imprinted on his memory .... His roses are a little like vegetables, it is true, ... but he is working to a price, and it will not do to be too critical.'

Barriers had been erected between industry and the artist, particularly in Britain: the pottery manufacturers jealously guarded the secrets of ceramic technology; the artist scorned the industrialist's means of production and scoffed at his lack of taste. During the second half of the nineteenth century, however, these prejudices were gradually eroded. A few firms not only consulted artists on matters of design and decoration, but also introduced the working practices of the studio into some departments of their factories. Through their association with the industry, some artists managed to glean enough technical information to set up their own potteries. At the same time there was a steady flow of manuals which described the processes involved in the production of pottery, and improvements were made in the accessibility and convenience of the necessary equipment and materials. As knowledge and experience grew, Arts and Crafts potters gained more and more independence from industry. Their greater aptitude enabled them to produce an ever wider range of effects, both creating and responding to changes in style and taste.

PAINTED POTTERY IN ENGLAND

A procedure in pottery making that is relatively simple and was therefore popular among amateurs, is decoration by means of painting with colours. The painting is done on pottery which has already been fired, and the colours need firing at only a comparatively low temperature. One of the earliest activities of Morris, Marshall, Faulkner & Co. was painting ceramic wall tiles, either for a decorative scheme or for selling in the Firm's shop. William Morris made several designs for tiles, although he actually painted very few himself. Philip Webb and Edward Burne-Jones, among others, supplied designs, and at least some of the painting was done by Kate and Lucy Faulkner, sisters of Charles

Faulkner. The blank tiles were bought from commercial manufacturers in Holland.

In 1868 the Grill Room of the South Kensington Museum (now the Victoria and Albert Museum) was decorated to designs by the artist Edward Poynter. His scheme included a large area of tiles which were painted by lady students of the National Art Training School (now the Royal College of Art). Such was the success of this exercise that it was decided to establish a studio for china painting, on a site near the Albert Hall in Kensington Gore. The Staffordshire firm of Minton, who had fired the Grill Room tiles, agreed to provide staff and equipment, and in 1871 Minton's Art Pottery Studio was opened under the direction of the watercolour artist William Stephen Coleman.

As well as the students of the National Art Training School, many painters, professional and amateur, availed themselves of the opportunity to work in a different and challenging medium. George W. Rhead, a Minton employee who worked at the Art Pottery Studio, recorded: 'Nearly everybody took up pot-painting for a time, and a considerable business was done .... in the supply of materials and firing. It was indeed more than a craze; it became a positive fever.'

Minton's Art Pottery Studio was burnt down in 1875, but the china-retailers Howell & James arranged alternative facilities for firing amateurs' work and organized annual competitions which continued into the 1880s. Most china painted by the myriad amateurs, large quantities of which have survived, was in the form of tiles, plaques or pilgrim-bottles, all of them shapes which offer large,

flat surfaces for decoration. The subject chosen was, more often than not, flowers; otherwise, there were genre scenes, figures (often in medieval costume), animals and almost direct copies of Italian maiolica and English delftware. The pottery was usually treated as if it were a canvas or a sheet of paper; decorative borders and reserved panels (common features of most painted china decoration) were hardly ever used.

Rookwood pottery vase decorated by Sara Sax
Height: 23.6cm
Sold: Sotheby's, New York, 11/6/87
Price: $1045

The Doulton factory at Lambeth, London, began in about 1874 to produce painted ware which the firm called 'Faience'. Some of the artists whom Doulton employed had gained experience at Minton's Art Pottery Studio, but the particular technique adopted at Lambeth had been developed by John Bennett who had joined the firm about 1873. Such was the success of the Doulton Faience shown at the Philadelphia Centennial Exposition of 1876 that Bennett decided to emigrate to the USA. By 1878 he had set up a studio in New York and was offering tuition in china-painting. For a year he gave classes at the city's Society of Decorative Art. Most of his decoration was floral, but he also imitated Persian and Rhodian wares.

AMERICAN PAINTED POTTERY

There was a strong contingent of amateur china-painters in Cincinnati. Instruction had been given at the University School of Design since 1874 and, like the woodcarving course started the previous year, the classes were attended largely by young ladies from Cincinnati's wealthier families. Among the students was Mary Louise McLaughlin who developed 'Cincinnati Limoges', a type of painted pottery made in imitation of the French *barbotine* ware, examples of which were shown at the Philadelphia Centennial. This technique, used at the time by potteries in the area round Limoges in France, involved painting on the clay body with coloured slip (liquid clay), which produced a textured effect like oil painting. Both china-painting and the *barbotine* technique flourished among the ladies of Cincinnati. Kiln facilities were provided by local manufacturers until 1880 when Maria Longworth Nichols opened the Rookwood Pottery in an abandoned schoolhouse on Mount Adams.

The access to ceramic technology afforded Mrs Nichols by the Dallas Pottery during the months before she started her own concern, is a striking instance of crumbling walls between industry and the artist. Although the Rookwood decorators used the *barbotine* technique, the coloured slips were increasingly refined until the decoration looked almost like any

Vase by Rookwood Pottery
Height: 13.7cm
Michael Carey Inc., New York
Price: $175

other underglaze painting. Flowers, birds and insects were the commonest decorative motifs, and the decoration and its treatment were on the whole Japanese in feeling. The Rookwood Pottery rapidly became a successful commercial venture. Some examples of Rookwood fetch enormous sums at auction, but such was the quantity and quality of the pottery's output that it is quite possible to find very good pieces at more modest prices.

Much rarer than Rookwood are examples of the *barbotine*-painted pottery made by Charles Volkmar, who succeeded Bennett as instructor at the Society of Decorative Art in New York. Volkmar was a painter who had been trained in France. On his return to America, he set up a studio at Greenpoint, New York, and made pottery usually painted with

landscapes, in the style of the Barbizon school of artists. He used coloured slips made from ground porcelain which he obtained from the Union Porcelain Works nearby.

LUSTRE WARE

A further class of pottery with painted decoration was the lustre ware made by William de Morgan and others. Towards the end of the 1860s de Morgan began experimenting with lustre glazes, and by the mid 1870s, working in Chelsea, he mastered the technique of creating silver, gold and copper lustre glazes.

About 1872 de Morgan had availed himself of the facilities at Minton's Art Pottery Studio, where, no doubt, he had scrutinized equipment and quizzed technicians. There, he would also have had the opportunity to develop the Persian colours (blue,

**Lustre tile
by William de Morgan**
15.2 × 15.2cm
Richard Dennis, London
Price: £200

Tile by Morris & Co.
15.2 × 15.2cm
Richard Dennis, London
Price: £100

green, puce) that he sometimes used as an alternative to lustres.

At first William de Morgan bought tiles, dishes and pots from commercial firms, which he then decorated. But in 1882 he moved his works to Merton Abbey, where he made his own tiles and employed a man to throw pots to his designs and under his supervision.

De Morgan used a number of decorative motifs, ranging from floral patterns not unlike some of Morris's work, to apocryphal beasts and birds, inventions of his own quirky imagination. Peacocks, eagles,

Lustre vase by Pilkington's
Height: 30.5cm
Sold: Phillips, London, 18/6/87
Price: £506

**Copper lustre tiles
by William de Morgan**
9.7 × 40cm
Sold: Phillips, London, 18/6/87
Price: £715

leopards, serpents, many and varied galleons, and even classical subjects appear on his pottery.

Most of de Morgan's vases and plates, except for very small or badly fired pieces, are beyond the means of the average collector, but tiles are more affordable. Generally, other factors equal, lustre-decorated examples are more expensive than those painted in Persian colours.

One of the potteries from which de Morgan bought blanks was Craven Dunhill, of Jackfield in Shropshire. They and another firm in the same area, Maw & Co., produced wares, including tiles, decorated with copper lustre in styles derived from de Morgan's work. Although technically accomplished, their lustre ware was artistically less successful than de Morgan's. Maw & Co, however, manufactured pieces designed by Walter Crane and Lewis F. Day, which are quite distinguished. Walter Crane supplied designs for lustre decoration to the Pilkington Tile & Pottery Co. of Clifton Junction, near Manchester, as well. From 1903 this firm produced lustre ware decorated in a variety of styles. Heraldic motifs, often incorporating mottoes or quotations, were used, as were figure subjects, animals, fish and flowers, usually formalized to some extent.

John Pearson, who was employed for a while by de Morgan and subsequently worked in copper with the Guild of Handicraft and the Newlyn Industrial Class, made pieces of lustre ware independently at some stage in his crowded career. He painted commercial blanks with designs in silver and gold lustre, usually depicting galleons, animals or fish, in a rather crude style.

Lustre vase by Pilkington's
Height: 24.8cm
Richard Dennis, London
Price: £750

SALT-GLAZED STONEWARE

In 1852, following London's third cholera epidemic in twenty-one years, the British parliament passed the London Water Act. This provided for the hygienic supply of water through salt-glazed stoneware pipes. The huge contract for their manufacture was awarded to the Lambeth firm of Doulton & Co. John Sparkes, headmaster of the local art school, prevailed on Henry Doulton, in about 1865, to devote some of the profits from this contract to the manufacture of art pottery, to be designed and decorated by his students.

In 1867 the firm's artistic stone-ware won critical acclaim at the International Exhibition in Paris, and there were further successes at exhibitions in London during the early 1870s. Art studios were opened at the factory in 1873, and several students from the Lambeth School of Art were taken on as decorators. Most of the new employees were young women who, in 1882, recorded their gratitude to Henry Doulton in an illuminated address: 'The Lady Artists and Assistants', they gracefully declared, '.... take this opportunity of expressing our obligations to you for the origination of an occupation at once interesting and elevating to so large a number of our sex.'

Stoneware vase
by the Martin brothers
Height: 9cm
Richard Dennis, London
Price: £320

Stoneware vase
by the Martin brothers
Height: 16cm
Richard Dennis, London
Price: £280

Doulton's artistic salt-glazed stoneware was incised, carved and modelled with decorative designs, mostly of flowers and animals. Throwing or firing salt-glazed stoneware is particularly dificult: the clay body is less plastic than earthenware, and glazing with vapourized salt requires a very high temperature and great experience in order to be able to judge the critical moment when the salt has to be thrown into the kiln. On the other hand, it is an excellent medium of artistic expression, since the glaze is so thin that the artist's every touch and scratch is visible in the finished article.

Salt-glazed stoneware was also produced by the firm of C.J.C. Bailey at the Fulham Pottery in London. Its output included jardinières designed by the architect John Pollard Seddon.

Bailey's kiln was also used to fire the work of the Martin brothers who, from 1873, made stoneware at Pomona House nearby. Robert Wallace Martin, the eldest brother, was a young sculptor who had trained at

Vase by Brannam Pottery
Height: 50.5cm
Sold: Phillips, London, 18/6/87
Price: £286

the Lambeth School of Art and had worked as a modeller at the Fulham Pottery. Walter and Edwin Martin had both been employed for a time at Doulton's. By 1877 the brothers had amassed enough technical knowledge to set up their own pottery at Southall, Middlesex; their work was decorated with flowers, fish, dragons or Renaissance ornament.

Robert Martin modelled tobacco-jars in the form of weird birds (sometimes comic, sometimes sinister), grotesque hybrids which served as toast-racks or spoon-warmers, and more representational figures of humans and animals. Walter Martin was a thrower and chemist, and he eventually developed an unprecedented range of colours for salt-glazing. He was also in charge of firing the kiln, a haphazard and often dramatic procedure. Edwin Martin's activities were at first limited to incising and colouring the decoration, but in about 1895 he started decorating pots with stripes, spots, hatching, veining and feathering, generally derived from markings found on flora or fauna.

The Martin brothers' stoneware was sold at the Artificers' Guild in Maddox Street, London; both Nelson Dawson and Edward Spencer were avid collectors of Edwin Martin's work. Robert Martin's birds and grotesques generally fetch very high prices (the record is over £47,000). Large, well-decorated vases are also very expensive, but some smaller items (most of Edwin Martin's work) are more affordable.

Susan S. Frackelton of Milwaukee, Wisconsin, also made salt-glazed stoneware decorated with incised designs of flowers. Her progress in the field of ceramics from china-painting to stoneware was much facilitated by having a father who owned brickyards and a husband who ran a business importing pottery and glass. She was probably already acquainted with Doulton's art pottery by 1874, when she began to experiment with salt-glazed stoneware. Her work was fired at traditional stoneware potteries in Minnesota and Ohio.

Elton vase
Height: 51 cm
Sold: Phillips, London, 24/3/87
Price: £242

SGRAFFITO WARE

The success of Doulton's salt-glazed stoneware alerted aspiring potters to the decorative possibilities of manipulating the clay body of the vessel, rather than merely treating it as a surface for painting. In Barnstaple, Devon, the architect Alexander Lauder founded a pottery in the late 1870s which produced *sgraffito* ware. By this process, the fired vessel is covered with a layer of slip in a different colour, through which the decorative design is incised. It had been a traditional form of decoration on Devon pottery for centuries, but Lauder used designs governed by current taste, incorporating elements of Renaissance and Japanese ornament.

Charles Hubert Brannam, who from 1879 ran one of his father's two Barnstaple potteries making traditional crockery, also switched production to artistic wares decorated with *sgraffito* designs. His output was much greater than Lauder's, and he used a wide variety of decorative motifs, although fish swimming through swirling water became a staple design from the mid-1890s.

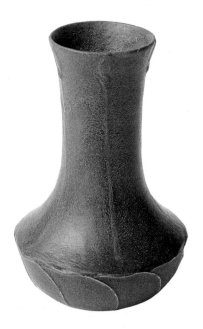

Vase by Grueby Pottery Co.
Height: 18.8cm
Michael Carey Inc., New York
Price: $1175

Vase by Pewabic Pottery
Height: 10.6cm
Michael Carey Inc., New York
Price: $900

106

ELTON AND OHR

Sir Edmund Elton started making pottery in 1879 on his estate at Clevedon, near Bristol, with the assistance of his gardener, who threw the pots to his directions. Like the Barnstaple potters, Elton decorated his work with slip, but he used a different method. He applied pieces of stiff slip to his vessels, which he carved into flowers and leaves. Frequently he distorted his pots into strange, sculptural shapes, sometimes with multiple handles or elaborate spouts. In this respect Elton's work is curiously parallel to the pottery made by George Ohr in Biloxi, Mississippi. Ohr also distorted his vessels and often applied elaborate handles. The Mississippian, however, was a virtuoso thrower and modeller, a Paganini of the clay vessel, whereas Elton's pots have much thicker walls. Ohr hardly decorated his pottery, relying on mottled and metallic glaze effects. Elton, too, developed metallic glazes; from 1902 he covered his pots with crackled gold and platinum lustres.

THE INFLUENCE OF CHINESE GLAZES

During the second half of the nineteenth century, potters in Europe and America emulated the fine monochrome glazes found on Chinese ceramics of the seventeenth and eighteenth centuries, particularly the deep red known as *sang de boeuf* (ox blood). At first the endeavour was restricted to large factories such as those at Sèvres and Berlin, which had the necessary technical and financial resources. Then individual potters took up the challenge.

Hugh Cornwall Robertson, with his

Jug by George Ohr
Height: 8.8cm
Sold: Phillips, New York, 27/6/87
Price: $1320

father and brother, ran the Chelsea Keramic Art Works at Chelsea, Massachusetts, where earthenware with modelled decoration was made to designs by, among others, the cabinetmaker Isaac E. Scott. In 1876 Hugh Robertson saw Chinese monochromes at the Philadelphia Centennial Exposition and began a long series of experiments in the hope of matching them. Using a stoneware body, he achieved a *sang de boeuf* (which he called 'Robertson's blood'), deep sea- and apple-greens, a mustard yellow and a turquoise.

In 1889 Robertson ran out of funds and the pottery had to be closed. But two years later, with financial backing from several Boston connoisseurs, he re-opened his works as the Chelsea Pottery. There he developed a crackled white glaze, again copied from Chinese ceramics, on which decorative designs were painted in cobalt blue. At first he used motifs derived from Oriental blue-and-white, but then patterns of stylized animals or plants were adopted. This ware proved very popular and a number of designers and decorators worked on it. It was mostly made at the Dedham Pottery in Dedham, Massachusetts, where Robertson moved in 1896.

Charles Fergus Binns also tried to copy Chinese monochrome glazes on stoneware when he was in the United States. His many years at the Royal Worcester Porcelain Co. in England, where his father was manager, had given him a knowledge of most of the various techniques involved in manufacturing ceramics. He recognized the importance of the individual being able to control the entire process, and he was the first to teach this approach to pottery. One of his earliest students, Mary Chase Perry, also decorated her pottery with glaze effects. She opened the Pewabic Pottery at Detroit in 1903, and with her partner Horace J. Kaulkins and a small staff made pots and tiles covered in lustrous glazes in a range of colours, including black, tan, lavender and turquoise.

The Fulper Pottery Company of Flemington, New Jersey, was an old-established firm which made utility vessels in stoneware. In about 1900, it too began producing pots and lamp-bases covered in glazes inspired by Oriental ceramics. The company made a speciality of a crystalline glaze which it called 'Leopard Skin'.

There were three principal English potteries engaged in experiments with Oriental glaze effects. The Doulton factory in Burslem, Staffordshire, developed a deep red glaze which it named 'Flambé'. Then Bernard Moore started his own workshops with a small staff of decorators, at nearby Stoke-on-Trent, where he ex-perimented with Oriental glazes, using stoneware and porcelain bodies. The glazes he achieved were typically deep red, vivid yellow and turquoise, sometimes combined with lustres, and decorated with designs of fish, bats, peacocks, galleons, plum blossom and other subjects, often with an Oriental flavour. A brief period spent working for a firm of Staffordshire porcelain manufacturers gave William Howson Taylor the expertise to set up his own pottery at West Smethwick, near Birmingham, in 1898. He produced stoneware vases, bowls and bottles covered with glaze effects inspired by Oriental ceramics, particularly reds, greens and purples, usually mottled or streaked.

RELIEF DECORATION IN THE UNITED STATES

During the 1890s there emerged in the United States a number of potters who decorated their work with low relief carving, or modelled it in the round. In many cases this sculptural pottery was covered in a matt glaze; this combination can be traced back to the wares exhibited by the French potter Auguste Delaherche in 1893 at the World's Columbian Exposition in Chicago.

Particularly close in style to some of Delaherche's work was the pottery manufactured by the Grueby Faience Company of Boston. Many of the firm's pots were designed by the architect George Prentiss Kendrick, between 1897 and 1901. To vases in classic Oriental forms were applied filets of clay which the Grueby decorators modelled into the stylized plant and foliate forms designed by Kendrick. The vessels were then usually covered in a matt green glaze, although other colours were used occasionally and sometimes petals or buds were picked out in yellow.

Kendrick was succeeded at Grueby by another architect, Addison LeBoutillier, who designed some excellent tiles decorated in low relief with stylized trees. The stature of Grueby pottery was increased when Stickley included it in exhibits of his Craftsman furniture.

Teco Art Pottery, made by the Gates Potteries of Terra Cotta, Illinois, was also generally covered in a matt green glaze, but paler and more even than that found on Grueby wares. Vases, jardinières and lamps were designed by William Day Gates who ran the firm. Some Teco vases were modelled in an Art Nouveau style by the sculptor Fernand Moreau. Gates also commissioned designs from Frank Lloyd Wright,

William B. Mundie and other Chicago architects, which are in the geometrical style of the Prairie School.

Other artists whose work was characterized by modelling and matt glazes include two former Rookwood artists, who independently set up their own potteries in the West: Artus Van Briggle and Albert Valentien. Van Briggle had been one of Rookwood's most promising designers, and the firm had sent him to study art in Europe. On his return he made some vases for Rookwood with figurative decoration, but his work was interrupted by tuberculosis. In 1899 he went to Colorado where he stayed until his death five years later. In 1902 he set up the Van Briggle Pottery Company at Colorado Springs, and the moulded vessels produced there were decorated with figures or flowers in high relief and

Plaque by Rookwood Pottery
Width: 60.5cm
Sold: Sotheby's New York, 5/12/86
Price: $1320

covered in matt glazes. His wife continued the pottery after his death, eventually selling up in 1910. The new owners continued to use Van Briggle's moulds for many years after his death.

Albert Valentien had been the first decorator employed by the Rookwood Pottery on a regular basis. In 1908 he and his wife (another Rookwood decorator) retired to San Diego, California, and opened a pottery in 1911. They had to close it two years later when the neighbours complained about the smoke, but in the short period of its existence the Valentien Pottery produced vessels decorated, like Van Briggle's, with figures and flowers modelled in relief. The Art Nouveau style of the

pottery recalled Mrs Valentien's studies in Paris under Rodin at the turn of the century.

The tiles produced at the works set up by Ernest A. Batchelder in 1909 at Pasadena, California, were also decorated in relief, with a wide range of subjects, including motifs drawn from Gothic art and Mayan ornament, and Californian flora and fauna.

Other American ceramics with sculptural decoration were made by Tiffany Studios, Mary Louise McLaughlin (who produced 'Losanti' ware) and Adelaide Alsop Robineau (who produced carved and pierced porcelain). These are all very rare and expensive, to be admired in museums rather than collected. With

Teco Pottery vase
Height: 16.4cm
Michael Carey Inc., New York
Price: $1500

Vase by Van Briggle Pottery
Height: 10.6cm
Michael Carey Inc., New York
Price: $900

her husband, Adelaide Robineau ran *Keramic Studio* from 1899, a magazine which provided a forum where American potters could share technical information and aesthetic ideas. She had studied under Binns and became a member of the remarkable team assembled by E.G. Lewis at the University City Pottery, Ohio, which included the French potter Taxile Doat and the Englishman Frederick Hurten Rhead (G.W. Rhead's nephew); the enterprise had only been going two years when in 1911 Lewis was investigated for fraud, and the team was dispersed.

RELIEF DECORATION IN BRITAIN

There was not much pottery made in Britain with relief decoration, apart from some of the salt-glazed stoneware made by Doulton and the Martins. The Della Robbia Pottery, founded in 1894 at Birkenhead near

Plaque by Della Robbia Pottery
29 × 49cm
Sold: Phillips, London, 24/3/87
Price: £572

Liverpool, by Harold Rathbone (cousin of the metalworker R.L. Rathbone), produced low-relief panels. These were modelled by, among others, Conrad Dressler, Ellen Mary Rope, Robert Anning Bell and Rathbone himself. Vases, jars and pitchers were usually decorated with patterns of flowers or figures (often putti) which were incised and painted; knobs and handles were sometimes modelled as human or animal figures. The Compton Pottery, established near Guildford, Surrey, around 1902 by Mary Seton Watts (wife of the painter George Frederick Watts), produced garden pottery with moulded decoration inspired by Celtic ornament.

MATT-GLAZED WARE

After 1900 the character of American painted pottery altered in response to changing taste. The shiny, glassy glaze that had covered the painted decoration was replaced by matt and semi-matt glazes. The Rookwood Pottery introduced what it called 'Vellum' ware; other potteries which used matt glazes also conventionalized the decoration, usually plants, birds or animals.

Typical of work in this style was the ware produced by the Newcomb College Pottery established at New Orleans, Louisiana, in 1895, although matt glazes were not used there until 1911. The decorators were women students at the College, which was affiliated to Tulane University. Their work was supervised by Mary Given Sheerer, formerly a decorator at the Rookwood Pottery, who was employed by the College. The pottery was incised and painted with decorative designs of stylized local flora and fauna.

From 1907 the same sort of ware was made by the Saturday Evening Girls Club which met at the North End branch of the public library in Boston, Massachusetts. This venture, which was founded to give some employment to the daughters of poor immigrant families, was called the Paul Revere Pottery, and it produced a wide range of utility wares as well as decorative vases.

Matt glazes with conventionalized designs was a decorative effect particularly favoured by former pupils of Binns. Paul Cox, who introduced matt glazes at Newcomb College, had studied at Alfred, and so had Arthur E. Baggs who took charge of the Marblehead Pottery founded in 1904 at Marblehead, Massachusetts. The flowers, animals, insects and landscapes painted in matt colours on the ware produced at this pottery were sometimes so stylized as to be virtually abstract. At about the same time, another of Binns's students, Frederick E. Walrath, made similar pottery at Rochester, New York. From 1911 Elizabeth Overbeck, who had also studied at Alfred, made pottery with her sisters at their home in Cambridge City, Indiana, which they decorated with designs of conventionalized flowers, incised and painted in colours under a transparent matt glaze.

**Panel decorated by
Robert Anning Bell**
58.8 × 32.6cm
Sold: Phillips, London, 24/3/87
Price: £275

Vase by Rookwood Pottery
Height: 21.5cm
Michael Carey Inc., New York
Price: $525

**Bowl by Saturday Evening Girls'
Club**
Diameter: 18.3cm
Michael Carey Inc., New York
Price: $400

**Vase by Newcomb College
Pottery**
Height: 15.3cm
Michael Carey Inc., New York
Price: $1500

Vase by Rookwood Pottery
Height: 26.6cm
Michael Carey Inc., New York
Price: $525

Vase by Paul Revere Pottery
Height: 16.3cm
Michael Carey Inc., New York
Price: $1500

EARLY TWENTIETH-CENTURY BRITISH CHINA-PAINTING

In Britain, too, painted pottery was given a new lease of life in the early years of the twentieth century. In 1903 Alfred Powell began painting pottery for the Wedgwood factory. He married Louise Lessore in 1906 and she also started painting Wedgwood pottery. They worked in various styles, Alfred Powell painting landscapes, architecture, flora and fauna, and Louise specializing in armorial designs which sometimes incorporated lettering. Some designs were painted in silver and copper lustre. Other artists who occasionally painted for Wedgwood in similar styles were the architects H. Thackeray Turner and W.R. Lethaby, and Grace Barnsley, Sidney Barnsley's daughter. Alfred Powell taught china-painting at the Central School of Arts and Crafts in London, and he trained Millicent Taplin who ran a studio at the Wedgwood factory where a handful of decorators were employed painting in the style that the Powells had initiated.

Therese Lessore, Louise Powell's sister, painted pottery for Wedgwood during the 1920s. Her style was related to work by painters of the Bloomsbury Group such as Duncan Grant and Vanessa Bell. The Omega Workshops, the Bloomsbury Group's contribution to the Arts and Crafts Movement, had produced pottery between 1913 and 1916 painted by both Grant and Bell, which is, however, very rare.

In 1914, in order to gain more technical expertise, Roger Fry, the founder of the Omega Workshops, had contacted the firm of Carter &

Wedgwood dish painted by Alfred Powell
Diameter: 46.3cm
Richard Dennis, London
Price: £550

Tiles by Carter Stabler Adams, designed by Harold Stabler
46 × 46cm
Malcolm Haslam
Price: £650

**Stoneware group of St George
and the Dragon
by Adrian Allinson**
Height: 35.5cm
Sold: Sotheby's, London, 4/6/87
Price: £605

Co. at Poole, Dorset, which had recently started to produce pottery with painted decoration. After the First World War, Carter's formed a subsidiary company called Carter Stabler Adams, the principals of which were Cyril Carter, Harold Stabler the metalworker, and John Adams, who had worked for a time with Bernard Moore. The newly-formed concern made vessels and tiles painted in colours on a crackled white slip with designs of flowers, birds and animals in a style which approaches Art Deco.

THE INFLUENCE OF EARLY CHINESE POTTERY

In 1910 the Burlington Fine Arts Club held an exhibition in London of early Chinese pottery. This was the first comprehensive display of stoneware from the Tang and Sung dynasties (seventh to thirteenth centuries AD), and it had an immense and immediate effect on British artist-potters. The sculptor Reginald Wells, who had previously been making slipware in the style of the seventeenth century, began to emulate the work of the early Chinese potters, producing footed vessels with handles in the form of small lugs. George Cox, working at his Mortlake Pottery in London, made vessels often decorated with dragons, incised or modelled in high relief, and covered with glazes inspired by Tang and Sung pottery. In 1913 Cox left England to

**Wedgwood plate
painted by Therese Lessore**
Diameter: 23.5cm
Richard Dennis, London
Price: £250

take up an appointment at Teachers College, New York, where he taught pottery making. At Rainham in Kent the Upchurch Pottery was opened in 1913 and produced pottery designed by Edward Spencer in the style of early Chinese wares.

However, these first attempts to copy early Chinese ceramics were frustrated by lack of technical expertise. They were earthenware fired at a comparatively low temperature and it was not until after the First World War that stoneware was covered in felspathic glazes, the authentic materials of Sung dynasty wares.

William Staite Murray had been trained at the Camberwell School of Arts and Crafts where the brothers Alfred and Henry Hopkins, former employees at Doulton's, taught the full range of ceramic techniques and

118

**Stoneware vase
by William Staite Murray**
Height: 7.1cm
Malcolm Haslam
Price: £300

procedures. Murray, in Rotherhithe near London, began making pots in the manner of early Chinese ceramics at about the same time as Bernard Leach, trained in Japan by a traditional stoneware potter, produced a similar ware at his pottery in St Ives, Cornwall.

FIGURE MODELLERS

A number of artist-potters working in Britain during the 1920s made ceramic figures. Harold and Phoebe Stabler were the precursors of a school of Arts and Crafts figure modellers working in London. There was the painter and sculptor Adrian Allinson, a teacher at the Central School, who used stoneware for his lightly stylized figures of humans, animals and birds. Working in Chelsea was a group of figure modellers which included Gwendoline Parnell (a former pupil at the Camberwell School of

Arts and Crafts), Harry Parr and Charles Vyse. They made figures modelled in exquisite detail and minutely painted; among their subjects were gypsies, street-vendors, eighteenth-century ladies of fashion, and characters of pagan mythology. At Lamorna, Cornwall, the jeweller Ella Naper made figures, many of them portraits of herself and her friends.

In America, pottery figures were made at the Cowan Pottery Studio in Rocky River, a suburb of Cleveland, Ohio. R. Guy Cowan, who had studied under Binns at Alfred, produced the figures and vessels using a white porcelain clay. In 1925 he was joined by Arthur E. Baggs, formerly director of the Marblehead Pottery, who introduced a wider range of better-quality glazes. From 1928 the Studio produced limited editions of figures modelled by sculptors such as Paul Manship, Waylande Gregory and A. Drexler Jacobsen. The painter Carl Walters made pottery figures of animals, birds and fish at his workshop in Woodstock, New York, from 1922, decorated with abstract patterns.

STAINED GLASS

By way of a postscript, a brief mention must be made of the enormous quantities of stained glass, ecclesiastical and domestic, which were produced in Britain and America by artists of the Arts and Crafts movement. Such prominent figures as William Morris, Frank Lloyd Wright and Charles Rennie Mackintosh designed stained glass windows. Examples of their work appear very rarely on the market and tend to fetch astronomical prices. Windows by lesser artists, and even anonymous pieces, are also very expensive if they have any pretension to artistic quality.

Object	Quality of Manufacture	Quality of design and/or decoration	Rarity	Price (£)	Price ($)
Batchelder, E.					
Tile	8	8	■■	30–50	55–90
Carter Stabler Adams					
9-tile panel designed by H. Stabler	8	9	■■■	600–800	1050–1400
Vase	8	8	■	50–150	90–265
Cowan Pottery Studio					
Figure	8	8	■■	500–900	875–1575
Dedham					
Painted plate/vase	8	8	■■■	800–1000+	1400–1750+
De Morgan, W.					
Lustre/'Isnik' vase	8	9	■■	700–1000+	1225–1750+
Lustre tile	8	9	■■	200–400	350–700
'Isnik' tile	8	9	■■	150–300	265–525
Fulper					
Vase	8	8	■■	200–600	350–1050
Grueby					
Vase	8	8	■■	500–1000+	875–1750+
Leach, B.					
Vase	8	8	■■	350–1000+	615–1750+
Martin Brothers					
'Gourd' vase	8	8	■■	250–800	440–1400
Vase with fish/flower decoration	9	8	■■	300–1000+	525–1750+

Quality on a scale 1–10   ■ Rare   ■■ Very rare   ■■■ Extremely rare

Object	Quality of Manufacture	Quality of design and/or decoration	Rarity	Price (£)	Price ($)
Moore, B. Bowl	8	8	■■	250–500	440–875
Morris & Co. Painted tile	7	9	■■	100–150	175–265
Murray, W.S. Vase	9	8	■■■	250–750	440–1315
Newcomb College Vase	8	8	■■	600–1000+	1050–1750+
Ohr, G. Vase/Jug	9	8	■■	500–1000+	875–1750+
Paul Revere Pottery Vase	7	8	■■	600–1000+	1050–1750+
Pewabic Vase	8	7	■■	500–1000+	875–1750+
Pilkington Lustre vase	8	8	■■	300–900	525–1575
Pleydell-Bouverie, K. Vase	9	8	■■	250–750	440–1315
Rookwood Vase	8	8	■■	500–1000+	875–1750+
Vase (matt glaze)	7	7	■	400–800	700–1400
Van Briggle Vase	7	8	■■	500–1000+	875–1750+

Quality on a scale 1–10   ■ Rare   ■■ Very rare   ■■■ Extremely rare

THE BOOK
OF THE
ROYCROFT
ERS

CHAPTER FOUR

BOOKS

The Book of the Roycrofters
Roycroft Press, cloth-backed
boards designed by Dard Hunter.
Sold: Phillips, New York, 27/6/87.
Price: $110

There is a bookish flavour to the whole Arts and Crafts movement. Literature is never very far away, whether it is the books from which the philosophy was drawn – Carlyle, Emerson, Ruskin – or the manuals, pamphlets and periodicals which the artists themselves wrote.

Some prominent figures of the Arts and Crafts movement were very successful authors as well, renowned in their own day as much for their literary output as for their artistic endeavours. The entry for William Morris in Chambers' Encyclopaedia of 1891 describes him as 'poet', and about seven eighths of the article are devoted to a discussion of his verse and prose; only the last sentence mentions his work as a designer and craftsman. William de Morgan was an obscure artist-potter until 1906 when he published *Joseph Vance* and immediately became a best-selling novelist. In America, one of the most celebrated leaders of the Arts and Crafts movement was Elbert Hubbard, founder of the Roycroft community, who was certainly an author rather than an artist.

MAGAZINES AND THEIR INFLUENCE

The Arts and Crafts movement resulted in a plethora of small magazines beng produced. Practically every group and guild issued a periodical of some sort, even if only for a brief period. The best-known ones are *The Hobby Horse* produced by the Century Guild, *The Dial* edited by Charles Ricketts and Charles Shannon, Gustav Stickley's *The Craftsman* and Elbert Hubbard's *The Philistine*. But there were lots of more obscure publications, such as *The Artsman*, a monthly issued by the

Rose Valley community near Philadelphia from October 1903 to February 1904, and George Wharton James's *Arroyo Craftsman*, published at Pasadena in 1909; only one number of this magazine ever appeared.

It was largely the design of these little magazines that encouraged commercial publishers and printers to pay greater attention to the appearance of their books. *The Hobby Horse* was published by George Allen who also published Ruskin's books. Herbert Horne, who contributed articles and ornament and drew the cover for the second series of the magazine, later designed type for both the Riccardi Press (the imprint of the Medici Society), and the Florence Press, started by the publishers Chatto & Windus in 1908. This is but a single instance of direct Arts and Crafts influence on printers and publishers, but there are many volumes issued during the late 1890s which indicate the trade's awareness of a growing taste among the public for well-designed books.

BOOK DESIGNERS

The role of the book designer – not just the illustrator – was at last taken seriously and a host of accomplished artists worked in the field. To give a few examples, in Britain there was Aubrey Beardsley who designed and illustrated books for Mathews & Lane, T. Fisher Unwin, J.M. Dent & Co. and other publishers. Charles Ricketts worked for John Lane, Ward Lock, Osgood McIlvaine & Co. and others. Lane also commissioned work from Jessie M. King and Laurence Housman; in addition, Housman worked for Macmillan and other publishers. Arts and Crafts architects who wrote books for commercial publishers often designed them as well: for example, C.F.A. Voysey's *Reason as a Basis for Art*, published in 1906 by Elkin Mathews, and M.H. Baillie Scott's *Houses and Gardens*, issued the same year by Newnes.

The same complex web of designers and publishers spread itself across book production in America. Copeland & Day of Boston published books designed by Bruce Rogers, Bertram G. Goodhue and Tom B. Meteyard among others. Daniel B. Updike and William S. Hadaway both worked for Houghton Mifflin, another Boston publishing house. Will H. Bradley designed for Stone & Kimball of Chicago, Burrows Brothers of Cleveland and Frederick A. Stokes of New York; later he worked as art director on William Randolph Hearst's publications.

It would be impracticable to mention every Arts and Crafts designer who worked on books, or to list all the different publishing houses which employed them. What is significant is that the experience of working with commercial printers induced in some of the artists a desire to make their own books, and in both Britain and America private presses sprang up in profusion.

THE KELMSCOTT PRESS AND ITS INFLUENCE

The Kelmscott Press, the earliest of the private presses associated with the Arts and Crafts movement, was established in 1891 by William Morris. He had made earlier attempts to produce decorative books, which came to nothing, but in the late 1880s he became friendly with Emery Walker, partner in a photo-engraving business and an expert on all matters related to printing. With

The Nature of Gothic
by John Ruskin, Kelmscott Press
20.7 × 14cm
E. Joseph, London
Price: £350

Walker's advice and assistance, Morris designed and made his own type, which he called 'Golden' and which was based on fifteenth-century German originals used during the earliest years of printing. Unable to persuade any British manufacturer to supply him with black ink of sufficient density, he had to obtain it from the firm of Jaenecke in Hanover. He also bullied J. Batchelor & Sons of Little Chart in Kent into producing exactly the sort of hand-made paper that he wanted. Despite the fact that he was busy with other work, both artistic and political, and

printers. The book contains 87 wood-cut illustrations, engraved after drawings by Edward Burne-Jones, and numerous decorations by Morris. There were 425 copies printed on paper and 13 on vellum; many of them are now in museums. Any copy that comes on the market is inevitably very expensive. However, there are much cheaper Kelmscott Press books which, even if they are plainer, were made to the same high standards. Apart from Chaucer and Morris, the Kelmscott Press printed books by other authors including Wilhelm Meinhold, whose story *Sidonia the Sorceress* was translated by Lady Wilde, Oscar's mother.

Maud by Alfred Tennyson, Kelmscott Press
20.7 × 14cm
E. Joseph, London
Price: £420

Sidonia the Sorceress by W. Meinhold, Kelmscott Press
28.5 × 20.5cm
E. Joseph, London
Price: £750

although his health was failing, Morris managed to produce forty-two titles at the Kelmscott Press before his death in 1896. He designed 384 initial letters, 57 borders and 108 half-borders or marginal ornaments, and many of them he engraved on wood himself.

The finest book from the Kelmscott Press was *The Works of Geoffrey Chaucer*, completed in 1896, five months before Morris died. The folio size volume is printed in the 'Chaucer' type, a smaller version of the 'Troy' type which Morris had designed in 1892; like 'Golden' it was based on a font used by the early

❡ HERE BEGYNNYTH THE TREATYSE

OF FYSSHYNGE WYTH AN ANGLE

ALAMON IN HIS PARABLYS sayth that a good spyryte makyth a flourynge aege, that is a fayre aege & a longe. And syth it is soo: I aske this questyon, whiche ben the meanes & the causes that enduce a man in to a mery spyryte: Truly to my beste dyscrecion it semeth good dysportes & honest gamys in whom a man Ioyeth without ony repentaunce after. Thenne folowyth it that gode dysportes and honest games ben cause of mannys fayr aege and longe life. And therefore now woll I chose of foure good disportes & honeste gamys, that is to wyte; of huntynge: hawkynge: fysshynge: & foulynge. The beste to my symple dyscrecion whyche is fysshynge: callyd Anglynge wyth a rodde: & a lyne and an hoke. And therof to treate as my symple wytte may suffyce: both for the sayd reason of Salamon and also for the reason that phisyk makyth in this wyse. ❡ Si tibi deficiant medici medici tibi fiant: hec tria mens leta labor et moderata dieta. ❡ Ye shall understonde that this is for to saye, Yf a man lacke leche or med-

3

A Treatyse of Fysshynge ....
by J. Berners, Ashendene Press
19.5 × 13.5cm
E. Joseph, London
Price: £600

Some of those artists who contributed their skills to the production of the Kelmscott books were from Birmingham, where they also worked for the press run by the Birmingham Guild of Handicraft. Between 1894 and 1896 this press printed all six issues of *The Quest*, the Guild's magazine. The jeweller Arthur J. Gaskin, who later illustrated the Kelmscott edition of Edmund Spenser's *The Shephearde's Calender*, contributed woodcuts to *The Quest*, and Charles M. Gere, who designed many initials, ornaments and illustrations for the Birmingham magazine, had provided a frontispiece to an edition of Morris's *News from Nowhere*, printed by the Kelmscott

Press in 1893. That frontispiece had been engraved by W.H. Hooper, the craftsman who also engraved Burne-Jones's drawings for the Kelmscott Chaucer and many of the illustrations and ornaments in *The Quest*. An unusual feature of Birmingham Guild books was that both words and decoration were cut in wood; they were designed by Arthur Gaskin and Bernard Sleigh.

Charles Ricketts ran the Vale Press which lasted from 1896 to 1904. He was very much influenced by Morris's work at the Kelmscott Press, and there are many points of similarity between the two men's books. This was due in part to the fact that Emery Walker played the same role of friend and mentor to Ricketts as he had to Morris. Both men liked broad, dense borders, and the 'Vale' type that Ricketts designed was close to Morris's 'Golden'. But here similarities end and divergences begin, for Ricketts looked to sixteenth-century Italy for the models

127

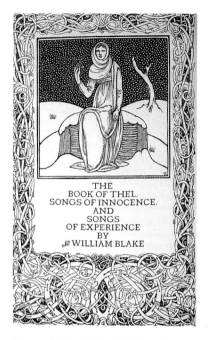

THE
BOOK OF THEL.
SONGS OF INNOCENCE.
AND
SONGS
OF EXPERIENCE
BY
WILLIAM BLAKE

The Book of Thel
by William Blake, Vale Press,
designed by Charles Ricketts
19.1 × 12.5cm
E. Joseph, London
Price: £200

---

on which he based his type rather than to the Germany of a century earlier. Ricketts' borders were printed from metal, not wood, permitting a finer line than Morris would ever have used.

Whereas the Kelmscott presses were installed in premises near Morris's home in Hammersmith and he did much of the printing himself with the help of only a small staff, Ricketts had his books printed at the Ballantyne Press, a firm of commercial printers, although the composition

and presswork were done under his personal supervision.

T. Sturge Moore who edited several of the Vale Press texts and illustrated the Vale *Wordsworth* was also associated with the Eragny Press. This was founded in 1894 by Lucien Pissarro, son of the Impressionist painter Camille Pissarro. When the younger Pissarro settled in England in about 1890, he soon made friends with Charles Ricketts who commissioned engravings from him for *The Dial.* Ricketts allowed him to use 'Vale' type for the Eragny Press books, although in 1903 Pissarro introduced his own 'Brook' type. With the assistance of his wife Esther, he developed a technique of printing woodcut illustrations in colours and sometimes gold leaf.

KELMSCOTT STYLE REJECTED

Nobody has disputed, then or now, the importance of William Morris to the Arts and Crafts revival of fine printing. From the Kelmscott Press all the others took their cue. There were, however, detractors who found Morris's printed page disagreeably crowded. Few would have gone as far as Max Beerbohm who ridiculed 'the muddled and fuddled, tame, weak, aimless, invertebrate and stodgy page done by Morris', but there were those who wanted greater clarity of design in their books than had been allowed by the density of type and decoration in the Kelmscott books.

One such was St John Hornby who started his press in the summerhouse of his family home at Ashendene, Hertfordshire, in 1895. For about four years it was a very amateur affair. Hornby, a director of W.H. Smith's the booksellers, was helped by his sisters and then his wife, and most of the type used was supplied by the Oxford University Press. In 1899 he moved to Shelley House, Chelsea, and soon organized what was still called the Ashendene Press on more substantial lines. Emery Walker and Sydney Cockerell (who had helped run the Kelmscott Press) designed for Hornby a font, 'Subiaco', based on a late fifteenth-century type. The spacing of letters and lines on the Ashendene page, and the calligraphic initials designed by Graily Hewitt, Louise Powell (the pottery painter) or Eric Gill, give Hornby's books an appearance quite distinct from the Kelmscott style, despite ideals and personnel shared by both presses. Charles Gere provided many illustrations to the Ashendene Press books, which were engraved in wood by W.H. Hooper.

If the ambition of the Ashendene Press was clarity, the Doves Press achieved austerity. This was the only private press in the running of which Emery Walker was actively engaged, and he designed what was probably his best type for its books. The other partner in the Doves Press, which was established at Hammersmith in 1900, was T.J. Cobden-Sanderson who was responsible for the selec-

Venus, regina Cnidi Paphique,
Sperne dilectam Cypron & vocantis
Ture te multo Glycerae decoram
Transfer in aedem.
Fervidus tecum puer et solutis
Gratiae zonis properentq; Nymphae
Et parum comis sine te Iuventas
Mercuriusque.

POSCIMUR. si quid vacui sub umbra
Lusimus tecum, quod & hunc in annum
Vivat et pluris, age dic Latinum,
Barbite, carmen,
Lesbio primum modulate civi,
Qui ferox bello, tamen inter arma
Sive iactatam religarat udo
Litore navim,
Liberum & Musas Veneremq; et illi
Semper haerentem puerum canebat
13

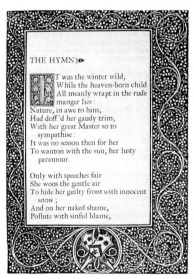

THE HYMN

IT was the winter wild,
While the heaven-born child
All meanly wrapt in the rude
manger lies :
Nature, in awe to him,
Had doff'd her gaudy trim,
With her great Master so to
sympathise :
It was no season then for her
To wanton with the sun, her lusty
paramour.

Only with speeches fair
She woos the gentle air
To hide her guilty front with innocent
snow ;
And on her naked shame,
Pollute with sinful blame,

Sapphica, by Horace,
Ashendene Press,
initials by Graily Hewitt
18.3 × 12.5cm
E. Joseph, London
Price (2 volumes): £950

Three Poems by John Milton,
Ashendene Press
21.8 × 16cm
E. Joseph, London
Price (subscription copy): £950

tion of texts and the bindings. There is no illustration in these books, nor are there any ornaments. A fine effect is achieved, however, by the perfect balance of Walker's type and the careful spacing of letters and lines. The compositor was John H. Mason who had begun his career in 1888 as a proof-reading boy at the Ballantyne Press. There he had met Charles Ricketts who had introduced him to Cobden-Sanderson. He taught printing and typography at the Central School of Arts and Crafts and was later appointed headmaster of the London School of Printing.

Another brilliant star in the Doves firmament was Edward Johnston who designed the initial letters and headings. Usually printed in red, sometimes in gold, these initials are a paradoxical mixture of grandeur and delicacy. Johnston, too, taught at the Central School (where Graily Hewitt was among his pupils), and in 1906 he published the very influential *Writing and Illuminating and Lettering*. The magnum opus of the press was the Doves Bible, printed in five volumes, which appeared between 1903 and 1905. All the Doves Press books are printed in the same type, laid out in the same style, and of only one size. Such uniformity induced Sir

Poems by Norman Davey, printed and bound at the Central School of Arts and Crafts
22 × 16cm
E. Joseph, London
Price: £450

Sartor Resartus by Thomas Carlyle, Doves Press, binding by T.J. Cobden-Sanderson
23.5 × 16.5cm
E. Joseph, London
Price: £950

**A Little Rosary by Gabriel
Pippet,
Pear Tree Press**
15.5 × 23cm
E. Joseph, London
Price: £70

Francis Meynell irreverently to describe them as literary Tiller Girls.

THE ESSEX HOUSE PRESS

C.R. Ashbee established the Essex House Press in 1898, with equipment and staff from the Kelmscott Press, which had finally expired that year. At first the type used was 'Caslon' which the Chiswick Press had revived earlier in the century. In 1901 Ashbee introduced the 'Endeavour' type which he designed himself. It is a thick type in the Kelmscott tradition and quite legible, despite several affectations typical of its designer. Many Essex House books were embellished with initials decorated with pinks, which were also designed by Ashbee. Illustrators included William Strang, Reginald Savage (who had contributed to *The Dial*), Paul Woodroffe, Edmund H. New (who had contributed to *The Quest*), T. Sturge Moore, Philip Mairet (Ethel Mairet's second husband) and Walter Crane, as well as Ashbee himself. Many of the illustrations were engraved by W.H. Hooper or Bernard Sleigh.

Ashbee's talent for making beautiful books was perhaps dissipated in the profusion of artists, engravers and compositors with whom he collaborated. Essex House was never a very 'private' press.

OTHER BRITISH PRIVATE PRESSES

The Pear Tree Press was the under-taking of a single individual, the artist James G. Guthrie. The press was established in 1899 at Ingrave in Essex, and it moved to Kent before it finally settled in 1907 at Flansham, Sussex. Guthrie designed, illustrated and printed most of the books himself and between 1902 and 1904 pro-duced four issues of *The Elf*, a maga-

THE PREFACE OF JOHAN BOURCHIER KNYGHT LORDE BERNERS, TRANSLATOUR OF THIS PRE-SENT CRONYCLE.

WHAT condygne graces and thankes ought men to gyve to the writers of historyes? Who with their great labours, have done so moche profyte to the humayne lyfe. They shewe, open, manifest and declare to the reder, by example of olde antyquite: what we shulde enquere, desyre, and folowe: And also, what we shulde eschewe, avoyde, and utterly flye. For whan we (beynge unexpert of chaunces) se, beholde, and rede the auncyent actes, gestes, and dedes: Howe, and with what labours, daungers, and parylls they were gested and done: They right greatly admon-est, ensigne, and teche us: howe we maye lede forthe our lyves. And farther, he that hath the perfyte knowledge of others joye, welthe, and highe prosperite: and also trouble, sorowe and great adversyte: hath thexpert doctryne of all parylles. And albeit, that mortall folke are marveylously separated, bothe by lande & water, and right wonderously sytuate: yet are they and their actes (done peradventure by the space of a thousande yere) compact togyder, by thistographier: as it were the dedes of one selfe cyte, and in one mannes lyfe. Wherfore I say that historie may well be called a divyne provydence: For as the celestyall bodyes above, complecte all and at every tyme the universall worlde, the creatures therin conteyned, and all their dedes: semblably so dothe history. Is it nat a right noble thynge for us, by the fautes and errours of other, to amende and erect our lyfe in to better? We shulde nat seke and acquyre that other dyd, but what thyng was most best, most laud-

B   i

Froissart's Cronycles,
Shakespeare Head Press
23.5 × 16.5cm
E. Joseph, London
Price (8 volumes): £850

---

zine which he both wrote and illus-trated. He sometimes used 'Caslon' type and sometimes 'Myrtle', a font designed by W. Herbert Broome, and he developed his own technique of printing in colours.

The story of the Shakespeare Head Press comes in two quite distinct chapters. The first covers the years 1904 to 1920 when the press was run by its founder A.H. Bullen whose ambition it was to print at Stratford-on-Avon the complete works of Wil-liam Shakespeare. He achieved this in ten volumes over three years; he

CHAPTER XI.

The Boy in the Rose Chemise.

YOU WILL REMEMBER A GIRL WHO HAD GONE DOWN TO Basrah for the Spring season among the captains, to whom Abu wrote, telling her of Mansur's. After a successful pil-lage this child, whose name was Sugar-of-Roses, came back

to the Blue Tavern and was pleased to love the poet as be-fore. But an old quarrel insisted between them, for, though Abu, as you will also remember, had denied any sort of heterodoxy in his love and had even urged the girl to return to box the ears of the new boy, his reputation remained,

54

Red Wise by E. Powys Mathers,
Golden Cockerel Press,
wood engraving by Robert
Gibbings
22 × 14.5cm
E. Joseph, London
Price: £80

also produced several other books before his death in 1920. Then the second part of the life of the Shakespeare Head begins. The press was bought by Basil Blackwell the Oxford bookseller, who employed Bernard H. Newdigate as designer. Previously, Newdigate had worked at the Arden Press in Letchworth, Hertfordshire, owned by W.H. Smith & Son. Interesting design was encouraged at the Arden Press where St John Hornby had some influence.

Newdigate's *chefs d'oeuvre* at the Shakespeare Head Press were editions of the works of Froissart, Chaucer and Spenser. Their refined beauty lies in the clarity of the 'Caslon' type used, the simplicity of Newdigate's design, the hand-drawn initials and occasional illustrations. A Shakespeare Head book of particular relevance to the Arts and Crafts movement was *Ernest Gimson, His Life and Work* by W.R. Lethaby, A.H. Powell and F.L. Griggs, published in 1924.

The Golden Cockerel Press was started in 1920 by Harold Midgeley Taylor as 'a co-operative society for the printing and publishing of books'. Taylor's idea was to print the work of contemporary writers and share any profits with them. But he soon found the plan impracticable and turned instead to the production of well-printed editions of classic texts. When Taylor died in 1925 the Golden Cockerel was taken over by the artist Robert Gibbings who at the time was working on woodcut illustrations for a book Taylor had been preparing. Gibbings concentrated on editions illustrated by his artist friends, among whom was Eric Gill who designed type, initial letters, borders and illustrations for several Golden Cockerel books. Other works were illustrated by John Nash, Mabel Annesley, John Farleigh, Eric Ravilious and David Jones.

It would be impossible to describe here the work of all the private presses that flourished in Britain during the first three decades of this century. However, their proprietors may be considered more or less adherents to the ideals of the Arts and Crafts movement to the extent that they followed the precepts set during the 1890s by William Morris at the Kelmscott Press.

PRIVATE PRESSES IN AMERICA

Morris's work was also the dominant factor in the revival of fine printing in America. The first Kelmscott book, *The Story of the Glittering Plain* by William Morris, was published in May, 1891, and only five months later Roberts Brothers of Boston, Morris's American publishers, issued a photographic facsimile. Another powerful influence on the early private presses in the United States was *The Hobby Horse*, the magazine produced by the Century Guild and printed at the Chiswick press. *The Knight Errant*, which was published quarterly at Boston from April 1892, was edited by Bertram Grosvenor Goodhue and Ralph Adams Cram, designed by Goodhue and printed by Francis Lee Watts at the Elzevir Press. Cram, an architect, later recalled: 'What we aimed to do was to take the English *Hobby Horse* and, in a manner of speaking, go it one better.' Although the quarterly resembles *The Hobby Horse* visually, it also embodied Kelmscott standards of book production. 'It was to be', wrote Cram, '.... a model of perfect typography and printer's art.'

By this time all were stoln aside
To counsel and undress the Bride;
But that he must not know:
But yet 'twas thought he ghest her mind,
And did not mean to stay behind
Above an hour or so.

When in he came (*Dick*) there she lay,
Like new-faln snow melting away,
('Twas time I trow to part.)
Kisses were now the only stay,
Which soon she gave, as who would say,
God Bw'y'! with all my heart.

8

A Ballad upon a Wedding
by Sir John Suckling,
Golden Cockerel Press, batik
cover (*left*) and wood engraving
by Eric Ravilious (*above*)
22 × 14.5cm
E. Joseph, London
Price: £140

Daniel Berkeley Updike founded the Merrymount Press at Boston in 1893, but the first book did not appear until 1896. It took Updike three years to complete *The Altar Book*. B.G. Goodhue designed the type, which was based on Morris's 'Golden', and the borders, which again are close to Kelmscott originals. The illustrations were drawn by the English artist Robert Anning Bell in a style reminiscent of Walter Crane's art. Although *The Altar Book* was composed at the Merrymount Press, the actual presswork was done by the firm of Theodore Low De Vinne in New York. One other Merrymount book appeared with borders designed by Goodhue (who this time also provided the illustrations), but after 1900 Updike's books became more restrained. He did, however, print a number of books with decorations designed by Herbert Horne who had worked on *The Hobby Horse*.

Two American presses of the 1890s in particular were characterized by their owners' enthusiasm for literature rather than the quality of the craftsmanship. Thomas Bird Mosher and Elbert Hubbard both printed texts which they believed should be read by everyone. Mosher was none too scrupulous about copyright and published several titles by contemporary British authors without obtaining permission or paying any royalties. His books were small; volumes in 'The Bibelot' series measure 20.6 × 10 cm (8¼ × 4 in). He generally used very little decoration, but produced two books in a style close to the work produced at the Kelmscott Press: Matthew Arnold's *Empedocles on Etna* and D.G. Rossetti's *Hand and Soul*.

Elbert Hubbard, who had visited the Kelmscott Press in 1892, founded the Roycroft community the following year at East Aurora, New York. He started printing books in 1896 and although at first his work was a little crude he soon achieved reasonable standards. It is difficult, however, to classify Roycroft as a private press because Hubbard's entrepreneurship meant that the community produced huge numbers of editions. The value of his books lies in the vast number of people they reached and the influence that they had on them.

There were several authentic private presses in America where standards of craftsmanship were never sacrificed to profitability. The Auvergne Press at River Forest, Illinois, was established in 1896 when William Herman Winslow, a manufacturer of ornamental iron and bronze, and Chauncey L. Williams, a partner in the Chicago publishing firm of Way & Williams, jointly purchased a press and some type. Their houses had been designed by Frank Lloyd Wright

UP IN THE MORNING EARLY.

UP in the morning's no for me,
Up in the morning early!
When a' the hills are cover'd wi snaw
I'm sure its winter fairly!

Cauld blaws the wind frae east to west,
The drift is driving sairly;
Sae loud and shrill's I hear the blast—
I'm sure it's winter fairly!

The birds sit chittering in the thorn,
A' day they fare but sparely;
And lang's the night frae e'en to morn—
I'm sure it's winter fairly!

4

Songs **by Robert Burns,
Golden Cockerel Press,
wood engravings by Mabel
Annesley**
22 × 14.5cm
E. Joseph, London
Price: £180

and the architect was soon involved in the decoration and even the presswork of the Auvergne books. Only two titles were printed – Keats's *Eve of St Agnes* and, in a much larger format, *The House Beautiful* by William C. Gannett. The latter has a lavish title-page embellished with elaborate geometrical decoration designed by Wright and inspired by the Oriental carpets that he collected.

Another press which favoured elaborate decoration was the Elston Press, founded in 1900 by Clarke Conwell. After one year in New York, Conwell moved to New Rochelle where the press remained until it was closed in 1904. Conwell has been described by the book designer Bruce Rogers as 'probably the most meticulous pressman who ever worked in the U.S.'. The decorative borders, designed by his wife Helen Marguerite O'Kane, combined elements of Beardsley, Burne-Jones and Japanese design. They were usually floral and well matched to the type being used, which was either 'Caslon' or 'Satanick' (the American Type Founders version of the Kelmscott typeface 'Troy').

Frederic W. Goudy was a prolific designer of types. The Village Press, which he established in 1903 at Park Ridge, Illinois, a suburb of Chicago, was largely created to make use of a font which he had designed, and which became known as 'Village' type. Unlike most other American types of this era, it was drawn entirely freehand. Goudy also designed borders for some Village Press books in a style derived from Morris. A few illustrations were included, most of them by W.A. Dwiggins. The compositor was Bertha Goudy, the proprietor's wife, whose contribution is a considerable part of the pleasing appearance of a Village Press page.

Dard Hunter's father owned a newspaper in Chillicothe, Ohio, and gave his son an early interest in fine printing by showing him a Kelmscott Press book. The young Hunter also heard about Elbert Hubbard, and in 1903 he joined the Roycrofters at East Aurora. He designed several Roycroft books which usually have title-pages decorated with flowers or trees stylized in the manner of the Glasgow designers. He left the Roycroft community in 1910 and travelled extensively in Europe. Eventually he returned to Chillicothe, and in 1915 set up the Mountain House Press there. Hunter worked quite independently, carrying out every process himself. He designed his own type, cut it and cast it, and made his own paper and ink. He was illustrator, compositor, printer and binder. Sometimes he was even the author as well, printing essays that he had written on the history and literature of papermaking. It seems appropriate to end this brief survey of the American private presses with such a complete fulfilment of the Arts and Crafts ideal, although more have been omitted than it has been possible to mention.

BINDERIES IN BRITAIN

The standard binding for private press books was made of plain paper-covered boards. There were, however, several binderies associated with the private presses in which individual volumes were bound, usually in leather-covered boards with tooled, inlaid and gilt decoration and lettering.

Thomas James Cobden-Sanderson started binding books in 1884 at the suggestion of Jane Morris, William Morris's wife, and he set up the Doves Bindery in Hammersmith nine years later. There he employed a small staff and, owing to his poor health, gave up binding himself. However, he continued to design bindings, many of them for Kelmscott Press and Doves Press books. An apprentice at the Doves Bindery called Douglas Cockerell became one of the leading artist-craftsmen in the field. He designed and made bindings for many books printed at the Ashendene Press and other private presses. Cobden-Sanderson's and Cockerell's bindings were generally in a floral or geometrical style related to Renaissance designs.

In 1902 a bindery was established at the Guild of Handicraft at Chipping Campden, Gloucestershire. It was run by Anastasia Power who had studied bookbinding under Cockerell at the Central School of Arts and Crafts. Some Essex House Press books were given very elaborate bindings which, for example, incorporated enamel plaques mounted in silver, and carved rosewood, holly or ebony. Leather bindings were generally decorated with a pattern of intersecting lines, sometimes incorporating ornament from the decoration of the text.

There were many individual binders, most of them women, among whom Sarah Prideaux and Katharine Adams were pre-eminent. Cedric Chivers, too, was well known. The Guild of Women-Binders had books printed specially for binding; Constance Karslake was the Guild's most talented designer. An equivalent organization for men was the Hampstead Bindery. Most of these binders used differently coloured leathers inlaid in ornamental designs usually

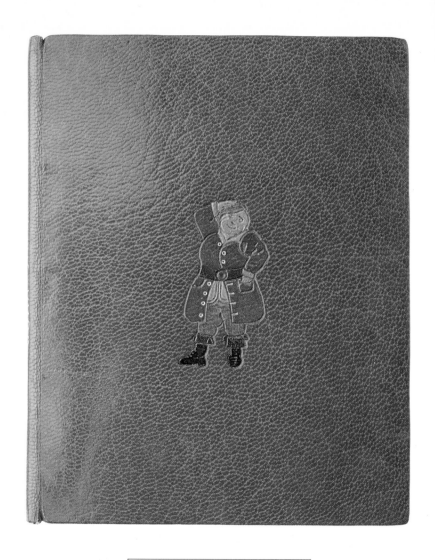

***John Gilpin* by W. Cowper,
inlaid leather binding by the
Guild of Women-Binders**
13.3 × 10.5cm
E. Joseph, London
Price (1st edition): £650

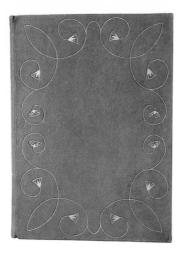

Songs from the Plays of Shakespeare
bound by the Guild of Women-Binders
20.8 × 15cm
E. Joseph, London
Price: £400

incorporating flowers and leaves, but sometimes depicting figures or landscapes treated in a pictorial manner.

AMERICAN BINDERIES

Roycroft books were bound at the community's own bindery, usually in chamois suede, known in the trade as 'limp ooze'. Unfortunately, this material has in many cases dried and crumbled over the years. Roycroft books were also sold in paper-covered boards, vellum, morocco or tooled leather. From about 1897 to 1911 the chief binder at Roycroft was Louis Herman Kinder who designed and made many fine bindings, which were usually decorated with geometrical patterns. For instance he might use green morocco, gilt tooled and inlaid with variously coloured leather.

Two outstanding American bookbinders were Ellen Gates Starr and Mary Crease Sears. Miss Starr had helped to introduce craftwork into the activities of Hull House, the settlement established by Jane Addams in 1889 to support the Chicago poor. In 1897 she went to London and studied bookbinding under Cobden-Sanderson at the Doves Bindery. Back in Chicago she set up a bindery in Hull House and took on apprentices. Her favourite pupil was Peter Verberg who soon became an accomplished binder himself. Miss Starr's style was naturally influenced by the work of Cobden-Sanderson and most of her designs comprise stylized flowers arranged in geometrical patterns.

Mary Crease Sears also studied bookbinding in London. On her return to the United States she set up a studio in Boston. Like Kinder at Roycroft she specialized in morocco covers inlaid with leather of different colours. One binding, which she exhibited at the Boston Society of Arts and Crafts in 1907, had covers of green morocco inlaid with a pattern of stylized irises and tulips made of more than a thousand pieces of variously coloured leather.

Object	Quality of manufacture	Quality of design and/or decoration	Rarity	Price (£)	Price ($)
Adams, K.					
Tooled morocco binding	9	8	■■■	300–600	525–1050
Ashendene Press					
Horace: *Sapphica* and *Alcaica* (2 vols)	9	9	■■■	800–1000	1400–1750+
J. Berners: *A Treatyse on Fysshinge*	9	9	■■■	500–750	875–1315
Central School of Arts and Crafts					
Tooled leather binding	8	8	■■■	300–600	525–1050
Chivers, C.					
Tooled calf binding inlaid with vellum and mother-of-pearl	9	9	■■	700–900	1225–1575
Cockerell, D.					
Tooled morocco binding with morocco inlays	9	9	■■	200–400	350–700
Doves Press					
T. Carlyle: *Sartor Resartus* bound by T. Cobden-Sanderson	9	9	■■■	900–1000	1575–1750
W. Shakespeare: *Coriolanus*	9	8	■■	300–500	525–875
Eragny Press					
Ronsard: *Choix de Sonnets* decorated by L. Pissarro	9	9	■■■	500–700	875–1225
Essex House Press					
J. Bunyan: *The Pilgrim's Progress* bound by A. Power	9	8	■■■	650–900	1140–1575
C.R. Ashbee: *The Masque of the Edwards of England*	8	8	■■	100–200	175–350

Quality on a scale 1–10   ■ Rare   ■■ Very rare   ■■■ Extremely rare

Object	Quality of manufacture	Quality of design and/or decoration	Rarity	Price (£)	Price ($)
Golden Cockerel Press					
J. de Breboeuf: *The Travels* illustrated by E. Gill	9	8	■■	400–600	700–1050
Guild of Women-Binders					
Tooled leather binding	8	8	■■	300–600	525–1050
Inlaid leather binding	9	8	■■	400–800	700–1400
Hampstead Bindery					
Tooled morocco binding	8	8	■■■	300–600	525–1050
Kelmscott Press					
A. Tennyson: *Maud*	9	8	■■	400–600	700–1050
J. Ruskin: *The Nature of Gothic*	9	9	■■	300–500	525–875
J. de Voragine: *The Golden Legend* illustrated by E. Burne-Jones	9	9	■■■	900–1000+	1575–1750+
Mosher, T.B.					
Bibelot (7 vols)	7	7	■■	50–100	90–175
Pear Tree Press					
G. Pippett: *A Little Rosary*	8	8	■■■	50–100	90–175
Roycroft Press					
E. Hubbard: *Will o' the Mill*	7	7	■■	50–100	90–175
Shakespeare Head Press					
Froissart: *Cronycles* (8 vols)	9	8	■■■	800–1000	1400–1750
G. Boccaccio: *Decameron*	9	8	■■■	500–700	875–1225
Vale Press					
W. Blake: *The Book of Thel* designed by C. Ricketts	8	9	■■	150–250	265–440

Quality on a scale 1–10   ■ Rare   ■■ Very rare   ■■■ Extremely rare

CHAPTER FIVE

JEWELLERY

Silver-gilt, jade, flawed emerald, moonstone and aquamarine brooch. John Jesse & Irina Laski, London. Price: £400

In 1867 diamonds were found near Hopetown in South Africa. Twenty years later, annual production at the five principal mines in the Cape Colony exceeded three and a half million carats, and a glittering cascade of diamonds started to pour over the rich women of Europe and America. During the last quarter of the nineteenth century the size and quantity of the diamonds worn by a woman became an accepted indicator of her husband's, father's or lover's wealth.

Arts and Crafts jewellers found the dominant position the diamond had assumed in jewellery disagreeable. Because of its sparkle and fire, a diamond demands attention and tends to dominate any ornament in which it is set, and the stone (and other precious stones like it) had become by far the most significant part of an ornament, the setting reduced until it was scarcely visible. The only craftsmanship to be seen was the actual cutting of the stone, a craft that lacked the humanity of either error or imagination (which were two qualities prized by the Arts and Crafts fraternity). Arts and Crafts jewellers looked instead to medieval and renaissance jewellery, where the overall design of the ornament was the first consideration, and gems took their place in the composition where they did not obscure the workmanship of the surrounding metalwork.

SEMI-PRECIOUS VERSUS PRECIOUS STONES

No less an authority (in the eyes of Arts and Crafts theorists) than John Ruskin had pronounced inexorably against any cutting of stones. The jewellers of the movement did not favour facet-cutting, which contributed to a stone's flash and sparkle but detracted from its colour and fire. So the diamond, colourless and inevitably facet-cut, was almost totally shunned. Cabochon-cutting however, was considered satisfactory. By this process the gem is polished until it is round and smooth; it gleams rather than glistens, and its colour is clear and regular.

Stones were chosen by Arts and Crafts jewellers for their aesthetic merits rather than their intrinsic value. At that time, diamonds, rubies, emeralds, sapphires and fine pearls were classed as precious, and most jewellery sold by the trade incorporated these stones. But they were used sparingly by Arts and Crafts jewellers, who favoured the semi-precious stones: amethyst, olivine, peridot, chrysoprase, carbuncle (cabochon-cut garnet), tourmaline, moonstone, spinel, turquoise and opal. In the comparatively rare instances when precious stones were used, they were often flawed or imperfect (Henry Wilson for example, chose heavily flawed emeralds for at least one piece of jewellery which he made.) This was partly a matter of cost, but also reflected the Arts and Crafts preference for individuality over uniformity. Similarly, whereas pure white, perfectly round pearls were used for fashionable jewellery, the Arts and Crafts jewellers preferred pearls that were yellow or grey, irregularly shaped and veined, and turquoises were used straight from the matrix, and were often much paler than the ones selected by commercial jewellers.

Other materials which Arts and Crafts jewellers used were enamels, pottery and glass, often in combination: C.R. Ashbee sang the praises of 'the green prismatic olivine .... on its field of blue enamel', and moonstones or pearls were combined with red enamel. The permutations were endless. If enamels were too bright for the overall composition of an ornament, then small pottery plaques, with their paler colours and softer tones, could be used. Glass or crystal beads, a feature of nineteenth-century Spanish and Italian peasant jewellery, were admired by the Arts and Crafts jewellers. Crystal was used for its 'twinkling' effect, to use Ashbee's epithet, by which he presumably wanted to imply something bright but less brilliant than diamonds.

Very little court jewellery was produced by the movement. There were one or two magnificent tiaras, but generally ornaments were not intended for ceremonial or even formal occasions. The necklace and pendant, one of the most usual forms of Arts and Crafts jewellery, would have been worn more in the evening than during the day. Other typical pieces

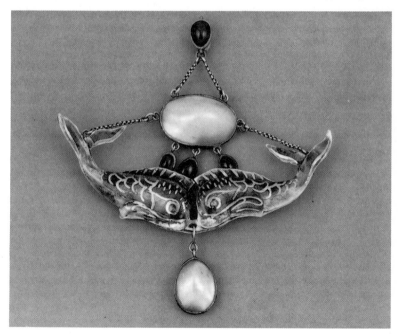

Mother of pearl, ruby and enamel pendant
Width: 8cm
Sold: Phillips, London, 18/6/87
Price: £484

Amethyst, pearl and mother-of-pearl pendant by Arthur Gaskin
Height: 6.5cm
Sold: Phillips, London, 21/10/86
Price: £440

were brooches and belt buckles. Small items were rarely made – very few rings and hardly any earrings. The aesthetic theory of Arts and Crafts jewellery demanded that one large piece should be worn to provide an obvious focus point in a person's appearance.

CLOTHING AND JEWELLERY

If the materials used for Arts and Crafts jewellery were dictated by a combination of aesthetic consideration and a regard for the means of those likely to buy it, the forms that it took were determined by the clothes that they wore. In the United States the American Free Dress League, and in Britain the Rational Dress Society, campaigned from the 1870s against the corset and in favour of looser, more practical garments for women. By the 1890s the sort of women who were involved with the Arts and Crafts movement wore either 'medieval' dresses (one of Liberty's best-selling lines), or some variation of a kimono (more popular in the United States), or else a full skirt, belt and blouse. This last costume became almost a uniform for women who held advanced views, and it explains the great number of buckles produced by the Arts and Crafts jewellers. Brooches were often worn to secure a shawl draped round the shoulders, or attached directly to the blouse in a central position.

**Silver and enamel buckle
by Omar Ramsden and
Alwyn Carr**
Height: 6.7cm
John Jesse & Irina Laski, London
Price: £500

**Chalcedony and blister pearl
pendant by the Guild of
Handicraft**
Height: 6.5cm
Sold: Phillips, London, 21/10/86
Price: £374

Dress reform was very much part of the Arts and Crafts ethos. *The Craftsman* ran several articles on 'plain and simple' clothes, and in England the Healthy and Artistic Dress Union included among the members of its committee Godfrey Blount and C.R. Ashbee's wife Janet.

ASHBEE AND THE GUILD OF HANDICRAFT

Ashbee was the first Arts and Crafts designer to turn his attention to jewellery. During the early 1890s the Guild of Handicraft produced ornaments such as buckles and brooches, which represented an extension of its metalworking activities. At first the craftsmen involved in creating the jewellery were the same as those

who had been making articles in copper and silver; few, if any, professional jewellers were taken on. So, not surprisingly, early pieces of Guild jewellery consisted of wrought or cast silver set with a few stones.

Gradually, as the craftsmen's skills developed, and as Ashbee's designs gained sophistication, more convincing pieces were made. Writing in 1894, Ashbee described his approach to the creation of jewellery: he designed it on paper, 'or with a piece of wire shaping curves that . . . . object to paper renderings; or with a piece of wax that will let itself be lovably pinched and petted, and holds the stones affectionately as you develop your work.' Combining the processes of design and execution, so that they act on each other, was an ideal which was seldom attained.

Ashbee's favourite stones were amethysts, carbuncles and pearls. They were set in silver, occasionally gold, and were often combined with enamels, either blue or red. His jewellery is often of staggering simplicity. From a single, semi-precious stone, a little silver and some silver wire, Ashbee could create a cheap, attractive ornament which was far removed from the typical, flashy trinket produced by the jewellery trade at that time. Much of the jewellery designed by Edgar Simpson is in a style closely related to Ashbee's simpler ornaments. Simpson's work was evidently identified with Ashbee's in one quarter; both artists were asked to show jewellery at the 1902 exhibition of the Vienna Secession.

Around 1900 the Guild of Handicraft took on several new craftsmen, some of whom were almost certainly trained jewellers. As well as simple pieces of jewellery, which went on being made, some much more elaborate ornaments were produced. They often involved a peacock, or sometimes the figure of a cherub cast in silver. These lavish creations represent Ashbee's attempts to emulate the achievements of his hero Cellini, perhaps the greatest goldsmith of the Italian Renaissance.

Enamelled pendant
Height: 5.5cm
Sold: Phillips, London, 19/6/86
Price (with brooch *en suite*): £143

WILSON AND HIS INFLUENCE

Unlike Ashbee, Henry Wilson thought Cellini 'an amazing blackguard'. Wilson looked to the eleventh rather than the sixteenth century for his model, and he chose for his handbook the *Diversarum Artium Schedula* by the monk Theophilus, which contains sections on metalwork and jewellery. Wilson's work was influenced by the forms of the buildings of Byzantium, and his ornaments often incorporate architectural and floral motifs in this style. The significance of his jewellery is disproportionate to the limited number of pieces that he created because he was very active as a writer and teacher. He was the first editor of *Architectural Review* which was started in 1896, he taught at the Central School of Arts and Crafts and the Royal College of Art, and in 1903 he published *Silverwork and Jewellery*, which became a standard manual on the subject.

It was in Wilson's workshop that John Paul Cooper picked up the rudiments of his craft. Cooper followed Wilson's style as closely in his jewellery as he did in his metalwork. Another jeweller who was powerfully influenced by Wilson was George Elton Sedding, son of Wilson's mentor J.D. Sedding. The younger Sedding was apprenticed to Wilson from 1901 to 1904 and three years later set up his own workshop in Noel Street, Soho, a part of London favoured by jewellers in those days.

THE ARTIFICERS' GUILD

Like John Paul Cooper and Henry Wilson, who supplied designs for jewellery and metalwork to the Artificers Guild, Edward Spencer designed jewellery for the Guild too, but it was less architectonic than theirs. It sometimes featured intricate arrangements of different coloured stones hanging on chains, and in this respect it is reminiscent of jewellery created by May Morris, one of William Morris's daughters. She sold her work at Montague Fordham's gallery in Maddox Street, which in 1903 became the retail premises of the Artificers' Guild.

John Houghton Maurice Bonnor, who worked in the architects' department of the London County Council and attended evening classes at the Central School, began collaborating with Edward Spencer in 1904 on some elaborate pieces of jewellery.

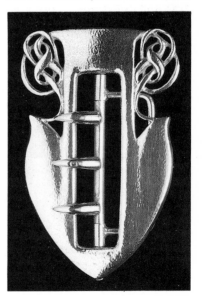

Silver buckle
Height: 6.1cm
John Jesse & Irina Laski, London
Price: £280

For instance, they designed together the 'Ariadne' necklace, made by craftsmen of the Artificers' Guild in 1905, which incorporated miniature figures of Ariadne, Eros and Anteros in three pendant lozenges, linked to a chain which consisted of alternate gold and silver plaques embossed and pierced as sailing ships. Bonnor set up his own workshop in about 1908 and later taught jewellery at the Camberwell School of Arts and Crafts.

ENAMELLISTS

Ashbee, Wilson, Cooper, Spencer and Bonnor occasionally used enamel in their jewellery, but it was used much more by Alexander Fisher and Nelson and Edith Dawson, the leading enamellists of the Arts and Crafts movement in Britain. The most famous piece was a girdle, by Alexander Fisher, made of wrought steel links set with semi-precious stones and plaques enamelled with scenes

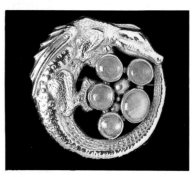

Gold and moonstone brooch attributed to John Paul Cooper
Height: 4cm
John Jesse & Irina Laski, London
Price: £900

from Wagner's operas. Fisher also made pendants and brooches, which always featured enamelled plaques. Nelson Dawson designed pieces of jewellery incorporating enamels made by his wife Edith, usually depicting birds, flowers or insects.

Carbuncle and enamel brooch
Height: 10cm
Sold: Phillips, London, 18/6/87
Price: £484

BIRMINGHAM JEWELLERS

There were strong connections between the Morris family and the Birmingham Arts and Crafts circle. Arthur Gaskin. who had been a student at the Birmingham School of Art, worked with Morris on Kelmscott Press books and towards the end of the 1890s took up jewellery. He worked with his wife Georgina, and their style is quite close to that of

May Morris; like her, they arranged coloured stones in compositions which are often evocative of the flowers featured on William Morris's fabrics and wallpapers.

From a series of evening classes organized by the Birmingham School of Art the Vittoria Street School for Jewellers and Silversmiths evolved. The new venture was supported by the Birmingham Jewellers and Silversmiths Association whose members released apprentices to attend classes. Arthur Gaskin was its headmaster from 1903 to 1924 when he retired to spend his remaining years at Chipping Campden in the Cotswolds. He was succeeded by William Thomas Blackband who had been one of the first apprentices to study at the School; he had won a scholarship to the Central School in London and in 1909 returned to Vittoria Street as an instructor. Blackband often collaborated with Gaskin on pieces of jewellery, using intricate techniques such as filigree and granulation. He made a speciality of the latter, claiming to have revived the skills of the ancient Etruscan goldsmiths.

Another product of the Vittoria Street School was Bernard Cuzner. The son of a watchmaker, he had been apprenticed to his father until he joined a firm of silversmiths in Birmingham. He attended classes at Vittoria Street and by 1901 was making jewellery in collaboration with Alfred H. Jones. Cuzner set up a workshop on his own and made metalwork and jewellery over the next fifty years. He taught metalwork at the Birmingham School of Art from 1910 to 1942, and it is as a silversmith rather than a jeweller that he is primarily remembered. However, his jewellery, influenced by Gaskin's work, is highly accomplished.

The Birmingham firm run by A. Edward Jones made some jewellery as well as silverware. Jones specialized in brooches set with ceramic plaques made by his friend William Howson Taylor at the Ruskin Pottery at West Smethwick, a suburb of Birmingham. He may also have made jewellery to designs by the Gaskins and other members of the Bromsgrove Guild which had been founded in about 1890 in another Birmingham suburb.

The Birmingham Guild of Handicraft seems to have made only a

**Silver and fire opal pendant
and chain**
Height (pendant): 6cm
John Jesse & Irina Laski, London
Price: £850

151

limited amount of jewellery. The Guild probably started producing it only after amalgamating with E. & R. Gittins Associated Craftsmen Ltd., in 1910. This Birmingham firm, organized more like an Arts and Crafts guild than a commercial company, made jewellery of high quality designed by H.R. Fowler.

Fred Partridge was the younger brother of Ethel Mairet the weaver, and like her attended the School of Art in their native Barnstaple, Devon. The story of his career as an Arts and

Liberty & Co. enamelled pendant
Height: 6.5cm
Sold: Phillips, London, 4/12/86
Price: £132

Crafts jeweller touches on many of the groups and institutions associated with the movement. Leaving his home town in 1899, Partridge studied for two years at the Birmingham School of Art. He then worked with the Barnstaple Guild of Metalworkers where he came into contact with Jack Baily, a craftsman with the Guild of Handicraft. In 1902 Partridge went to Chipping Campden and made jewellery for the Guild of Handicraft, but the following year he was dismissed by Ashbee for a moral misdemeanour. He went back to the Barnstaple Guild for a time and then took a post teaching at the Camberwell School of Arts and Crafts in London, where he preceded J.H.M. Bonnor. Around 1906 he set up a workshop in Branscombe in Devon. Ella Champion, one of his Camberwell students, joined him there. When the Branscombe venture was abandoned about 1910, Ella married Charles Naper and they went to live first at Looe and then at Lamorna, Cornwall, where there was a flourishing artistic community. Fred Partridge went to London and set up a workshop in Dean Street, Soho. After the First World War he joined Ethel Mairet at Ditchling, Sussex, where another artists' colony settled.

Partridge's career illustrates how a skilled craftsman could lead an almost itinerant life moving from one group to another in the complex network of the Arts and Crafts movement. Both he and Ella Naper were talented jewellers. They worked in a style which was, at least in part, derived from Lalique's art. In 1903 an exhibition of the Frenchman's jewellery was held at the Grafton Galleries, London, and there was another show of his work two years later at Agnew's also in London. Like Lalique, but exceptionally among British Arts and Crafts jewellers, Partridge and Naper often worked in horn. A comb by Ella Naper, for instance, in the form of a water-lily made of green-stained horn, set with moonstones representing droplets of water on its leaves, is very reminiscent of pieces by Lalique. However, there may have been a very different source for Partridge's horn combs. While living in Sri Lanka with her first husband Ananda Coomaraswamy, Ethel Mairet (Partridge's sister) took a great interest in Kandyan horn combs, publishing an article on them in a Sinhalese periodical.

NEWLYN AND KESWICK JEWELLERY

Two other institutions, the Newlyn Industrial Class and the Keswick School of Industrial Art, produced limited amounts of jewellery. At Newlyn it was mostly the work of Francis Charles Clemens, who attended a class in enamelling and silverwork started in about 1905 by the painter Reginald Dick. The pendants and brooches made by Clemens usually consisted of painted enamels depicting shells, fish or flowers and set in silver wirework. The general effect is reminiscent of the simpler jewellery made by the Guild of Handicraft. Among the instructors at the Keswick School of Industrial Art was the jeweller Herbert J. Maryon, who was probably responsible for most of the jewellery produced there. Like most of the Keswick metalwork, the jewellery was simple in design and unsophisticated in technique. Buckles and clasps predominated, which were usually made of silver and often set with turquoises.

JEWELLERY IN SCOTLAND

In Scotland, Herbert MacNair and his wife Frances Macdonald designed and made jewellery, but very little of it seems to have survived. Charles Rennie Mackintosh designed a famous silver pendant of birds flying across clouds formed from silver wire, with pendent seed pearls representing raindrops. This was made by Margaret Macdonald who sometimes collaborated on pieces of jewellery with her sister Frances. Talwin Morris also made jewellery, using much the same materials and techniques that he employed in his metalwork. His ornaments feature hand-beaten copper, silver or aluminium decorated with enamels and sometimes set with coloured glass. Phoebe Traquair, too, made pieces of jewellery, incorporating her enamel plaques to which she often gave titles, for example 'The Comforter', 'The Song' and 'The Mermaid'.

Two Scottish artists who specialized in jewellery were Mary Thew and James Cromer Watt. Mary Thew was a friend of Jessie M. King and her husband, the furniture and stained-glass designer E.A. Taylor; from early in the First World War they were near neighbours in Kirkcudbright. Her jewellery, which included brooches, pendants and tiny boxes, was made of silver, with materials such as abalone shell, semi-precious stones and enamels used on them pictorially. For instance, one of her brooches depicts a moonlit landscape in which the moon is a moonstone and the moonlight falling on the ground is abalone shell. Her work often has a silver ropework border. James Cromer Watt was a student at the Glasgow School of Art in about 1890 and later set up a workshop in

Liberty & Co. gold, opal and jadeite necklace
Length: 45.6cm
John Jesse & Irina Laski, London
Price: £980

Aberdeen. Like Thew, he made pendants, brooches and small boxes. He seems to have used gold to a greater extent than most Arts and Crafts jewellers, and he specialized in enamels enriched with *paillons* (inclusions of gold or silver foil). Sometimes his enamels were applied using the *cloisonné* technique.

**Gold, sapphire and moonstone
pendant by Liberty & Co.**
Height: 5cm
Sold: Phillips, London, 21/10/86
Price: £418

COMMERCIAL MANUFACTURERS

Several manufacturers of commercial jewellery included Arts and Crafts among the styles which they offered. Charles Horner of Halifax, Yorkshire, and three London firms – Murrle, Bennett & Co., Child & Child and Liberty & Co. – all produced large quantities of gold and silver jewellery which can be classified as either Arts and Crafts or Art

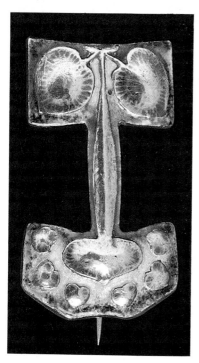

Liberty & Co. silver and enamel brooch
Height: 3.3cm
John Jesse & Irina Laski, London
Price: £280

Nouveau. Pieces which are more Arts and Crafts in character often feature enamels and silver made to look hand-beaten. Child & Child executed some designs for jewellery by the painter Edward Burne-Jones, and the firm produced quite competent enamelled pieces. Liberty & Co. bought designs from prominent Arts and Crafts jewellers, including Bernard Cuzner and Arthur Gaskin, but generally their more successful pieces were designed by artists who were not otherwise involved in jewellery. The firm's most accomplished designer was Archibald Knox, but as he seems to have conceived his jewellery in terms of mechanized production, it is difficult to ascribe to him a place in the Arts and Crafts movement. Jessie M. King's jewellery designs for Liberty's were only slightly, if at all, less distinguished than Knox's, and more in the Arts and Crafts style. They usually featured stylized flowers and birds against a background of interlaced strapwork, in the manner of ancient Celtic ornament. Ella Naper also supplied designs to Liberty & Co., and Edgar Simpson worked for a number of well-known manufacturers including Charles Horner.

JEWELLERY IN AMERICA

There seems to have been considerably less Arts and Crafts jewellery made in America than in Britain. It is not yet clear whether this is an accurate observation or is merely a reflection of the comparative lack of historical research undertaken to date. If there was a real dearth of American Arts and Crafts jewellery, two reasons might be suggested. First there was the enormous amount of jewellery manufactured by

Silver brooch
Width: 5.9cm
John Jesse & Irina Laski, London
Price: £240

Tiffany & Co. and other large firms, which may have satisfied the demands of customers inclined towards the Arts and Crafts taste. Second, the ethos created by Stickley's magazine *The Craftsman* had a strong streak of puritanism in it. The articles that the magazine carried dealing with women's attire urged simplicity and practicality; the rights and wrongs of even embroidered decoration were warmly debated, and jewellery was hardly mentioned at all.

The irony of American Arts and Crafts jewellery is that two artists, Louis Comfort Tiffany and Madeline Yale Wynne, could both subscribe to the same aesthetic credo yet produce totally different work. Mrs Wynne, who, like Tiffany, was trained as a painter, regarded making a piece of jewellery as composing in colour and form, and her choice of materials was made according to her artistic sensibility rather than the intrinsic value of the materials. She very often chose copper rather than gold or silver, and used rock crystal or pebbles rather than precious or even semi-precious stones. Tiffany, working in collaboration with Julia Munson who ran the jewellery department of Tiffany Studios from 1903, created totally different jewellery, although he started from the same premise. Using the semi-precious stones which had been exalted by the British Arts and Crafts jewellers, such as opals, garnets and amethysts, as well as enamels, Tiffany produced wonderfully opulent pieces, sometimes with a Byzantine density reminiscent of Henry Wilson's work.

Mrs Wynne's followers have been legion, although very often anonymous. Jewellery made out of hammered copper set with pebbles or enamels has been the stock in trade of Arts and Crafts jewellers, more or less skilled, from her day to this. In contrast, the jewellery produced by Tiffany Studios had no heirs when its manufacture was halted in 1916. There were, however, contemporary imitations. The New York firm of Marcus & Co. made jewellery which was sometimes very similar to Tiffany Studios' pieces. George E. Marcus, the firm's founder, exhibited jewellery designs at shows organized by the Boston Society of Arts and Crafts in 1897 and 1899.

Many of the silversmiths prominent in the American Arts and Crafts Movement also made jewellery. For instance, Clemens Friedell put to advantage his years of apprenticeship to a Viennese jeweller by making some pieces, usually in handwrought silver. Janet Payne Bowles made jewellery as bizarre as her

creations in silver. From the early 1900s silversmiths from Cleveland, Ohio, including Mildred Watkins and Horace Potter, made jewellery, usually of silver and often incorporating enamels.

Some of the most accomplished American Arts and Crafts jewellers were amateurs. Brainerd Bliss Thresher was a merchant and financier in Dayton, Ohio, who occupied his leisure hours making pieces of jewellery. His style was strongly influenced by Edward Colonna who spent three years designing rail car interiors for a Dayton company connected with Thresher's enterprises. Colonna subsequently became a leading Art Nouveau designer in Paris. Thresher often used carved horn for his jewellery, suggesting that he followed Colonna's career in

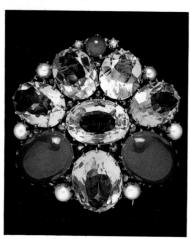

Silver, citrine, cornelian and pearl brooch
Diameter: 4cm
John Jesse & Irina Laski, London
Price: £300

Liberty & Co. silver and enamel cuff-links
Width: 2.5cm
John Jesse & Irina Laski, London
Price: £280

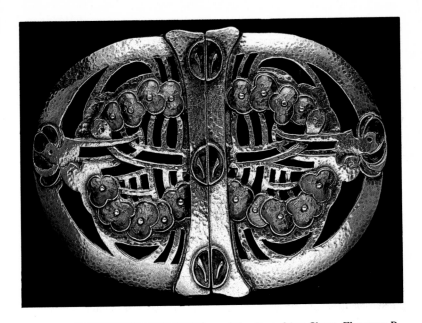

Liberty & Co. silver and enamel buckle designed by Jessie M. King
Height: 5.4cm
John Jesse & Irina Laski, London
Price: £850

France where horn was a material commonly used for jewellery.

Josephine Hartwell was already a trained artist and metalworker when she married the silversmith and sculptor Frederick A. Shaw. Mrs Shaw lived in Boston and made pieces of jewellery, 'the names of whose present owners', commented a writer in *House Beautiful*, 'would make my modest article take on the semblance of a Society Column'. Taught by the painter Arthur W. Dow, a connoisseur of Oriental art, she often incorporated antique Chinese jade carvings in her jewellery.

Like Josephine Shaw, Florence D. Koehler was a socialite. During the 1890s she painted china for the Rookwood Pottery. In 1897 she was in London where she studied enamelling under Alexander Fisher. Returning to Chicago she won a reputation for her jewellery, enamels and metalwork. Later, she lived in London and Paris. Her jewellery, mostly of gold, is finely crafted, often set with enamels, semi-precious stones and, particularly, pearls. Her style relates closely to the work of British Arts and Crafts jewellers. In London, she moved in artistic circles, counting many eminent painters among her friends. She won the plaudits of no less a critic than Roger Fry, who wrote in the *Burlington Magazine* of June 1910: 'It is in the imaginative and definitely poetic quality that Mrs Koehler's jewellery marks such an important moment in the modern revival of craftsmanship.'

159

Object	Quality of manufacture	Quality of design and/or decoration	Rarity	Price (£)	Price ($)
Anon.					
Silver buckle	7	7	■	200–400	350–700
Gold and moonstone brooch	8	7	■■	600–1000	1050–1750
Silver, citrine, cornelian and pearl brooch	8	8	■■	200–400	350–700
Silver brooch	7	7	■	100–300	175–525
Silver and fire opal pendant and chain	8	8	■■	750–1000+	1315–1750+
Silver and enamel pendant	7	8	■	100–400	175–700
Silver, pearl, mother-of-pearl, ruby and enamel pendant	8	8	■■	350–750	615–1315
Silver, carbuncle and enamel brooch	8	8	■■	350–700	615–1225
Silver and turquoise pendant	7	7	■	80–250	140–440
Brass and turquoise brooch	7	7	■■	40–80	70–140
Copper and enamel brooch	7	7	■	75–150	135–265
Artificers' Guild					
Silver, emerald and pearl pendant	8	8	■■■	600–1000	1050–1750
Birmingham Guild of Handicraft					
Silver buckle	8	8	■■■	200–400	350–700
Blackband, W.T.					
Gold, sapphire and pearl pendant	9	8	■■■	800–1000+	1400–1750+
Bonnor, J.					
Silver, mother-of-pearl and carbuncle pendant	9	8	■■■	750–1000+	1315–1750+
Child & Child					
Silver and enamel brooch	8	7	■■	350–700	615–1225

Quality on a scale 1–10   ■ Rare   ■■ Very rare   ■■■ Extremely rare

Object	Quality of manufacture	Quality of design and/or decoration	Rarity	Price (£)	Price ($)
Cooper, J.P.					
Silver and enamel brooch	9	9	■■■	800–1000+	1400–1750+
Dawson, N.					
Silver and enamel brooch	9	8	■■■	700–1000+	1225–1750+
Gaskin, A.					
Silver-gilt, amethyst and mother-of-pearl pendant	9	9	■■	400–800	700–1400
Silver-gilt, garnet, pearl and moonstone brooch	9	9	■■	500–1000+	875–1750+
Guild of Handicraft					
Silver, chalcedony and pearl pendant	8	7	■■	400–800	700–1400
Silver, ruby and enamel pendant	8	8	■■■	600–1000+	1050–1750+
Silver, turquoise and enamel brooch	8	8	■■■	500–1000+	875–1750+
Horner, Charles					
Silver and turquoise pendant	7	7	■	300–600	525–1050
Jones, A.E.					
Silver and 'Ruskin' pottery brooch	7	7	■	50–150	90–265
Keswick School of Industrial Art					
Silver and enamel brooch	8	8	■■■	250–750	440–1315
Koehler, F.D.					
Silver and enamel brooch	8	8	■■■	750–1000+	1315–1750+
Liberty & Co.					
Gold, opal and jadeite necklace	8	9	■■	900–1000+	1665–1750+
Silver and enamel buckle designed by Jessie M. King	8	9	■■■	750–1000	1315–1750
Silver and enamel brooch	8	8	■	200–600	350–1050

Quality on a scale 1–10   ■ Rare   ■■ Very rare   ■■■ Extremely rare

Object	Quality of manufacture	Quality of design and/or decoration	Rarity	Price (£)	Price ($)
Marcus & Co.					
Gold, emerald and enamel pendant	8	7	■■	600–1000+	1050-1750+
Murrle, Bennett & Co.					
Silver and enamel brooch	7	6	■	200–400	350–700
Naper, E.					
Horn comb	9	9	■■■	450–900	790–1575
Newlyn Industrial Class					
Silver and enamel brooch	8	8	■■■	200–400	350–700
Partridge, F.					
Horn comb	9	9	■■■	450–900	790–1575
Silver, ruby and pearl brooch	9	9	■■■	500–1000+	875–1750+
Ramsden and Carr					
Silver and enamel buckle	8	8	■	450–750	790–1315
Sedding, G.					
Silver and moonstone brooch	9	8	■■■	750–1000	1315–1750
Shaw, J.					
Silver and emerald brooch	9	8	■■■	800–1000+	1400–1750+
Thresher, B.					
Horn brooch	8	8	■■■	400–800	700–1400
Wilson, H.					
Silver, moonstone and enamel brooch	9	9	■■■	800–1000+	1400–1750+

Quality on a scale 1–10   ■ Rare   ■■ Very rare   ■■■ Extremely rare

Bibliography

Andersen, Timothy J., et al: *California Design 1910* (California Design Publications, Pasadena, 1974)

Anscombe, Isabelle, and Gere, Charlotte: *Arts and Crafts in Britain and America* (Academy Editions, London, 1978)

Berriman, Hazel: *Arts and Crafts in Newlyn 1890–1930* (Newlyn Orion, Newlyn, 1986)

Burke, Doreen Bolger, et al: *In Pursuit of Beauty* (MMA/Rizzoli, New York, 1986)

Cathers, David M.: *Furniture of the American Arts and Crafts Movement* (New American Library, New York, 1981)

Clark, Robert Judson, ed: *The Arts and Crafts Movement in America 1876–1916* (Princeton University Press, Princeton, 1972)

Collins, Judith: *The Omega Workshops* (Secker & Warburg, London, 1983)

Comino, Mary: *Gimson and the Barnsleys* (Van Nostrand Reinhold, New York, 1982)

Cooper, Jeremy: *Victorian and Edwardian Furniture and Interiors* (Thames & Hudson, London, 1982)

Crawford, Alan: *C. R. Ashbee* (Yale University Press, London, 1985)

Evans, Paul F.: *Art Pottery of the United States* (Scribner's Sons, New York, 1974)

Gooden, Susanna: *A History of Heal's* (Heal & Sons Ltd., London, 1984)

Haslam, Malcolm: *English Art Pottery 1865–1915* (Antique Collectors' Club, Woodbridge, 1975)

Johnson, Diane Chalmers: *American Art Nouveau* (Harry N. Abrams, New York, 1979)

Kaplan, Wendy: *"The Art that is Life": The Arts and Crafts Movement in America, 1875–1920* (Museum of Fine Arts, Boston, 1987)

Lambourne, Lionel: *Utopian Craftsmen* (Astragal Books, London, 1980)

Naylor, Gillian: *The Arts and Crafts Movement* (Studio Vista, London, 1971)

Richardson, Margaret: *Architects of the Arts and Crafts Movement* (Trefoil Books, London, 1983)

Rubens, Godfrey: *William Richard Lethaby* (Architectural Press, London, 1984)

Sanders, Barry, ed: *The Craftsman, an Anthology* (Peregrine Smith, Santa Barbara and Salt Lake City, 1978)

Index